THE YEAR YOU WERE BORN
1974

DEWAR'S "White Label" SCOTCH WHISKY

Welcome to Britain!

A fascinating book about the year 1974 with information on:
Events of the year UK, Adverts of 1974, Cost of living, Births, Deaths, Sporting events,
Book publications, Movies, Music, World events and People in power.

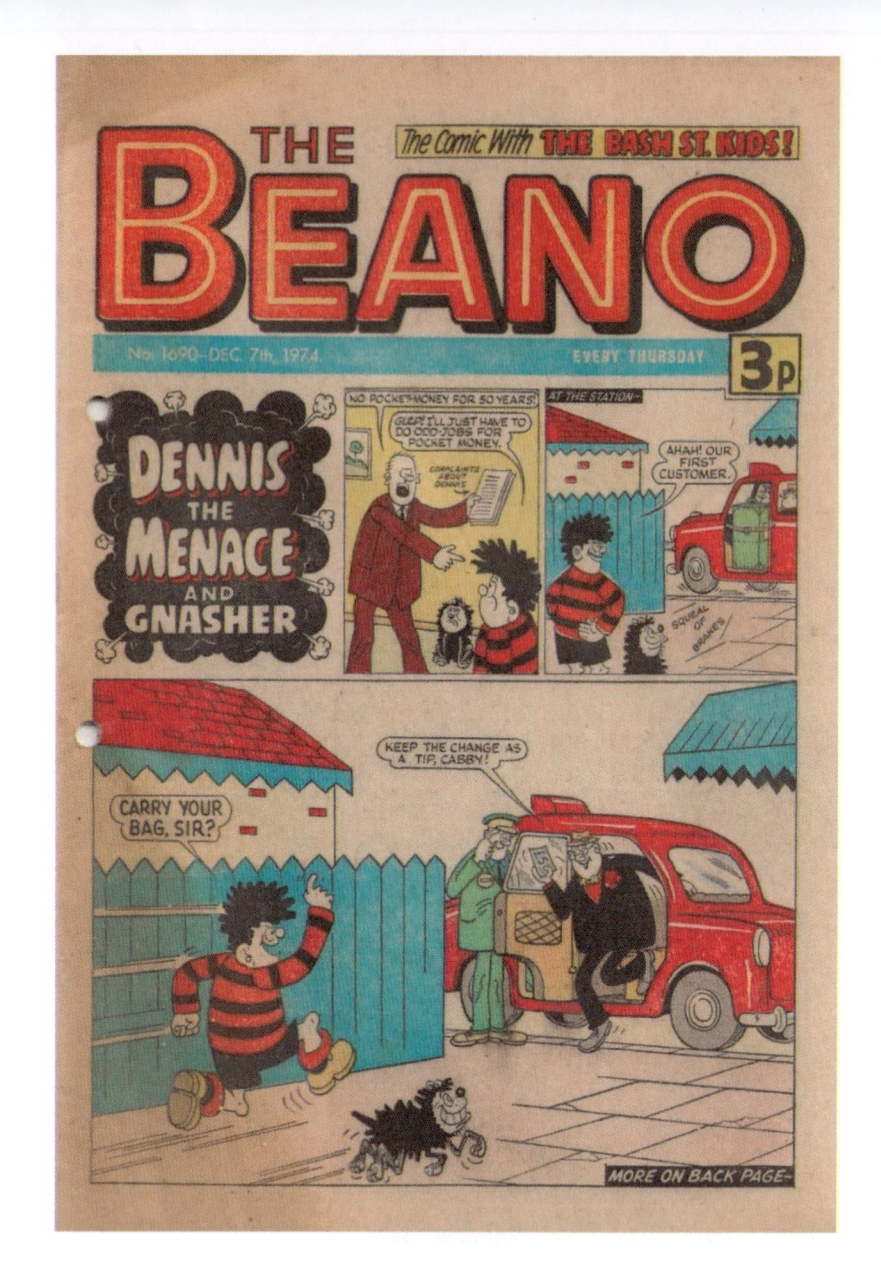

INDEX

Page 3	**Events of the year UK**
Page 14	**Adverts in 1974**
Page 22	**Cost of living**
Page 25	**Births**
Page 29	**Deaths**
Page 30	**Sporting events**
Page 38	**Book Publications**
Page 41	**Movies**
Page 54	**Music**
Page 64	**World Events**
Page 80	**People in power**

UK EVENTS OF 1974

January

1st — New Year's Day was celebrated as a public holiday in the United Kingdom for the first time nationwide, as England and Wales joined in making the first day of the year a paid legal holiday. Scotland had celebrated New Year's Day as a public holiday for years, and the order was applied to all of Britain by the 8th October amendment to existing wage laws.

4th — By a vote of 427 to 374, the Ulster Unionist Council in Northern Ireland voted to reject the Sunningdale Agreement that had been signed between the United Kingdom and the Republic of Ireland to establish a revival of the Northern Ireland Assembly and an advisory Council of Ireland with representatives from both Northern Ireland and the Republic.

7th — Former Northern Ireland Prime Minister Brian Faulkner resigned as the leader of the Ulster Unionist Party in the wake of the Party's January 4 rejection of the Sunningdale Agreement.

12th — Stephanie Britton, 57, and her 4-year-old grandson, Christopher Martin, were stabbed to death at their home on Hadley Green Road in the London Borough of Barnet. As of 2019 the case remained unsolved, although serial killer Patrick Mackay was a suspect.

16th — All 18 crew of the British cargo transport MV Prosperity were killed after the craft's engine failed and the vessel was driven onto the La Conchée Reef near Guernsey and sank. Only 16 bodies were recovered.

20th — For the first time in the history of English professional soccer football, a match in the The Football League was played on a Sunday. With a start moved to 11:30 in the morning to come before two other matches scheduled in the afternoon, Millwall defeated visiting Fulham, 1 to 0, in the League's Second Division. Striker Brian Clark of Millwall became the first English professional footballer to score a goal on a Sunday "when he drove the ball into the Fulham net at 11:34 a.m."

21st — The United Kingdom ended its embargo against delivering weapons to the Middle East. Arms deliveries had been suspended immediately after the Yom Kippur War broke out on October 6. Foreign Secretary Alec Douglas-Home informed the House of Commons that deliveries would be carried out, including "the supply of small arms and helicopters to Egypt and some naval equipment and spare tank parts for Israel."

24th — Prince Philip, Duke of Edinburgh, opened the 1974 British Commonwealth Games, known as "The Friendly Games", in Christchurch, New Zealand. They would continue until 2nd February.

January

27th | Three days before the second anniversary of the Bloody Sunday massacre of 13 civilians by British troops, 4,000 people participated in a peaceful protest march, organized by the Provisional Irish Republican Army. The march through Derry in Northern Ireland followed the route of the 1972 march.

31st | In Newtownabbey, County Antrim, a suburb north of Belfast, two armed robbers entered a workmen's hut and seized the week's wages of the 13 laborers inside. They then ordered the Protestants present to kneel on the floor. After two or three men did so, the gunmen opened fire on the other people in the hut, killing two Catholics (37-year-old Terence McCafferty and 29-year-old James McCloskey) and wounding three other men, including a Protestant. The gunmen were members of the Ulster Freedom Fighters.

February

1st | On the last day of the 1974 British Commonwealth Games in Christchurch, New Zealand, Tanzanian athlete Filbert Bayi set a new world record of 3 minutes 32.2 seconds in the 1500 metres event.

The bombing of a coach carrying off-duty British Armed Forces personnel and their families on the M62 motorway near Batley, England, killed nine soldiers and three civilians (including two children). The bombing was carried out by the Provisional Irish Republican Army, but the identity of the specific perpetrator or perpetrators remains unknown. Judith Ward was wrongfully convicted of the bombing in November 1974; her conviction was overturned in 1992.

7th | At midnight, Grenada became independent of the United Kingdom.

10th | All 260,000 coal miners in the United Kingdom went on strike as a result of a wage dispute with the National Union of Mineworkers.

12th | BBC One first airs the children's television series Bagpuss, made by Peter Firmin and Oliver Postgate's Smallfilms in stop motion animation. Despite 13 episodes being made, it becomes fondly remembered and gained a cult following.

February

14th | Bob Latchford, the Birmingham City centre forward, becomes Britain's most expensive footballer in a £350,000 move to Everton.

27th | Enoch Powell, the controversial Conservative MP who was dismissed from the shadow cabinet in 1968 for his "Rivers of Blood" speech opposing mass immigration, announces his resignation from the Conservative Party in protest against Edward Heath's decision to take Britain into the EEC.

28th | The general election results in the first hung parliament since 1929, with the Conservative government having 297 seats – four fewer than Labour, who have 301 – and the largest number of votes. Prime Minister Edward Heath hopes to form a coalition with the Liberal Party in order to remain in power.

March

1st | George Harrison announces his concert tour of US in November.

3rd | 180 Britons are among the dead when Turkish Airlines Flight 981 travelling from Paris to London crashes in a wood near Paris, killing all 346 passengers and crew on board.

4th | David Hares' "Knuckle" premieres in London.

Heath fails to convince the Liberals to form a coalition and announces his resignation as Prime Minister, paving the way for Harold Wilson to become Prime Minister for the second time as Labour forms a minority government.

6th | The miners' strike comes to an end due an improved pay offer by the new Labour government.

7th | The Three-Day Week comes to an end.

10th | Ten miners die in a methane gas explosion at Golborne Colliery near Wigan, Lancashire.

11th | Convicted armed robbers Kenneth Littlejohn and his brother Keith, who claim to be British spies in the Republic of Ireland, escape from Mountjoy Prison in Dublin.

15th | Architect John Poulson is jailed for five years for corruption. He was a British architectural designer and businessman who caused a major political scandal when his use of bribery was disclosed in 1972. The highest-ranking figure to be forced out due to the scandal was Conservative Home Secretary Reginald Maudling. Poulson served a prison sentence, but continued to protest his innocence, claiming that he was "a man more sinned against than sinning".

20th | Ian Ball fails in his attempt to kidnap HRH Princess Anne and her husband Captain Mark Phillips in The Mall, outside Buckingham Palace.

29th | The government re-establishes direct rule over Northern Ireland after declaring a state of emergency.

31st | British Airways becomes the unified brand for BOAC, BEA, Cambrian Airways and Northeast Airlines. The airline is the second largest UK-based carrier, based on fleet size and passengers carried, behind easyJet. In January 2011 BA merged with Iberia, creating the International Airlines Group (IAG), a holding company registered in Madrid, Spain. IAG is the world's third-largest airline group in terms of annual revenue and the second-largest in Europe.

April

1st | The Soviet car maker Lada, founded four years ago as a result of an enterprise by Italian automotive giant Fiat, begins selling cars in the United Kingdom: its 1200 four-door saloon is based on the Fiat 124 and retails for £999 (equivalent to £7,648.51 in 2022). They would be sold in Britain until 1997.

2nd | The Local Government Act 1972 comes into effect in England and Wales, creating six new metropolitan counties and comprehensively redrawing the administrative map. Newport and Monmouthshire are legally transferred from England to Wales.

England cricket fast bowler Tony Greig takes 8-86 in West Indies' 1st innings in tourists' 26 run 5th Test win in Port-of-Spain; Greig also captures 5-70 in 2nd innings.

6th | The 19th Eurovision Song Contest is held at the Dome in Brighton, produced and transmitted by the BBC. Katie Boyle hosts the event for the fourth time. Sweden wins the contest with the song "Waterloo", performed by ABBA, who become the first group to win the contest and go on to achieve huge international success.

8th | Paul McCartney & Wings release single "Band on the Run" in the US.

12th | The Annan Committee on the future of broadcasting is established to discuss the United Kingdom broadcasting industry, including new technologies and their funding, the role and funding of the BBC, Independent Broadcasting Authority and programme standards.

20th | The Troubles', the Northern Ireland conflict between republican and loyalist paramilitaries, British security forces, and civil rights groups, claims its 1000th victim.

24th | Leeds United win their second Football League First Division title.

27th | Manchester United are relegated from the Football League First Division where they have played continuously since 1938. Their relegation is confirmed when they lose 1–0 at home to their neighbours City in the penultimate game of the league season and the only goal of the game comes from former United striker Denis Law.

May

1st | Alf Ramsey, who guided the England national football team to victory in the 1966 FIFA World Cup, is dismissed by the Football Association after 11 years in charge.

May

2nd | The National Front gains more than 10% of the vote in several parts of London in council elections, but fails to net any councillors.

4th | Liverpool win the FA Cup for the second time, beating Newcastle United 3–0 in the Wembley final, with Kevin Keegan scoring twice and Steve Highway scoring the other goal.

6th | Inauguration of full electric service on British Rail's West Coast Main Line through to Glasgow.

8th | 50 MPH speed limit in Britain lifted.

17th | Ulster Volunteer Force (UVF) explode four bombs in Republic of Ireland, killing 33 civilians, wounding 300 (highest number of casualties in a single incident during "The Troubles").

20th | The Centre for Policy Studies, a Conservative social market think tank established by Keith Joseph, Margaret Thatcher and Alfred Sherman, holds its first meeting.

23rd | Great Britain performs nuclear test at Nevada Test Site.

24th | RCA releases "Diamond Dogs", David Bowie's 8th studio album, recorded in London and the Netherlands, with cover design by artist Guy Peellaert, it peaks in the U.S. charts at No. 5, and goes to No. 1 in the U.K. and Canada.

28th | Power-sharing in the Northern Ireland Assembly collapses following a strike by unionists.

29th | Television producer James MacTaggart, 46, dies unexpectedly of a heart attack before finishing the film Robinson Crusoe.

June

1st | 28 people are killed in the Flixborough disaster. The Flixborough disaster was an explosion at a chemical plant close to the village of Flixborough, North Lincolnshire, England on Saturday, 1st June 1974. It killed 28 and seriously injured 36 of the 72 people on site at the time. The casualty figures could have been much higher if the explosion had occurred on a weekday, when the main office area would have been occupied.

June

5th — Snow Knight wins the Epsom Derby at odds of 50/1 ridden by Brian Taylor.

8th — Jon Pertwee leaves Doctor Who in the final episode of Planet of the Spiders citing the death of his close acting friend Roger Delgado (who played 'The Master') the previous year as the reason. He is replaced by Tom Baker.

10th — The Queen's last surviving royal uncle, Prince Henry, Duke of Gloucester, dies at his home in Northamptonshire, seven years after his last public appearance. His funeral is held at Windsor Castle on 14th June.

15th — On 15 June 1974 the National Front held a march through central London in support of the compulsory repatriation of immigrants. The march was to end at Conway Hall in Red Lion Square. A counter-demonstration was planned by Liberation, an anti-colonial pressure group. During the late 1960s and early 1970s, the London council of Liberation had been increasingly infiltrated by hard-left political activists, and they invited several hard-left organisations to join them in the march. When the Liberation march reached Red Lion Square, the International Marxist Group (IMG) twice charged the police cordon blocking access to Conway Hall. Police reinforcements, including mounted police and units of the Special Patrol Group, forced the rioting demonstrators out of the square.

17th — A bomb explodes at the Houses of Parliament in London, damaging Westminster Hall. The Provisional Irish Republican Army (IRA) claims responsibility for planting the bomb.

20th — The remains of 17th-century naval vessel HMS Anne, on the low water mark of the beach near Pett Level, East Sussex, are designated under the British Protection of Wrecks Act.

22nd — A silent march retraces the route of the previous week's Liberation counter-demonstration from London's embankment to Red Lion Square, in memory of Kevin Gately.

24th — The government admits testing a nuclear weapon in the United States causing a rift in the Labour Party.

28th — Paul McCartney & Wings release singles "Band on the Run" and "Zoo Gang" in UK.

July

3rd | Don Revie, the manager of Football League champions Leeds United since 1961, accepts the Football Association's £200,000-a-year deal to become the new England manager.

4th | The UK's Northern Ireland Office publishes a white paper, The Northern Ireland Constitution, proposing elections to a body which would attempt to develop a political settlement for the country.

5th | British commercial diver John Dimmer suffers a pneumothorax during decompression while in saturation aboard the oil platform Sedco 135F in the North Sea. The diving supervisor recognizes the symptoms of pneumothorax, but the platform contacts an on-shore doctor who diagnoses Dimmer's condition as pneumonia. Dimmer's decompression continues, and he subsequently dies.

6th | Members of the failed Northern Ireland Executive and Northern Ireland Office (NIO) ministers hold talks in Oxford with Harry Murray, chairman of the Ulster Workers' Council (UWC).

12th | Bill Shankly, manager of FA Cup holders Liverpool, stuns the club by announcing his retirement after 15 years as manager. Shankly, 62, had arrived at Liverpool when they were in the Football League Second Division and transformed them into one of the world's top club sides with three top division titles, two FA Cups and a UEFA Cup triumph.

17th | 1974 Tower of London bombing: The Provisional Irish Republican Army (IRA) detonates a bomb at the Tower of London, in the UK, killing one person and injuring another 41.

20th | The first rock concert to be held at Knebworth House in Hertfordshire, UK, features The Allman Brothers Band, Van Morrison, Tim Buckley and others, and is attended by an estimated 60,000 people.

Leeds United appoint Brighton & Hove Albion manager Brian Clough, formerly of Derby County as their new manager.

21st | 10,000 Greek-Cypriots protest in London against the Turkish invasion of Cyprus.

26th | Liverpool appoint 55-year-old first team coach Bob Paisley as their new manager.

28th | Last production of steel by the Bessemer process in Britain, at Workington.

August

5th | Joan Jett forms her rock group Runaways in England.

15th | Collapse of Court Line and its subsidiaries Clarkson's and Horizon Holidays leaves 100,000 holidaymakers stranded abroad. On 15th August 1974, Court Line went bankrupt, with all flights cancelled, its fleet comprising two TriStars and nine One-Eleven 500s grounded, all 1,150 staff losing their jobs and as many as 100,000 holidaymakers stranded overseas with no means of getting home. To enable stranded holidaymakers to return to the UK at no additional cost to them, the collapsed group's rivals organised an airlift through the Tour Operators' Study Group (TOSG), the package holiday industry association. This operation was paid for using the £3.5m bond the failed group's tour operators had deposited with TOSG.

29th | Thames Valley Police break up the Windsor Free Festival.

September

2nd | ITV launches the sitcom Rising Damp starring Leonard Rossiter and Richard Beckinsale.

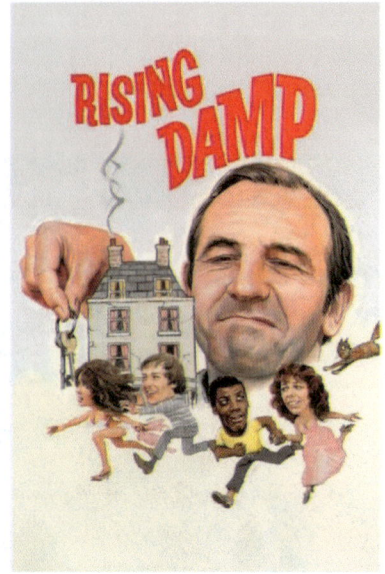

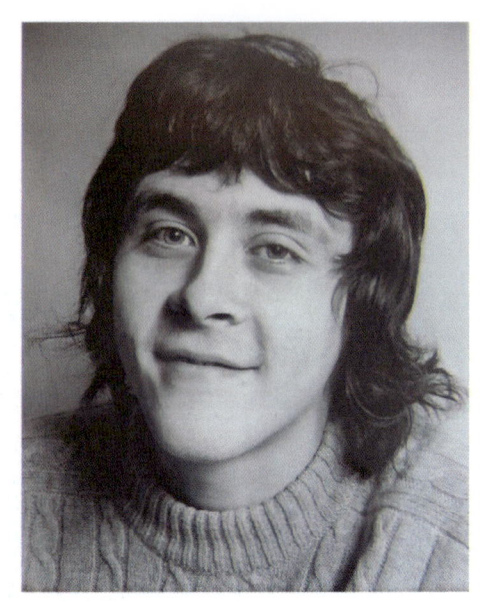

5th | ITV shows the feature-length pilot episode of The Six Million Dollar Man, starring Lee Majors as the half-man, half-cyborg action hero Steve Austin.

Following the pilot shown in April 1973, BBC1 commences with the Ronnie Barker prison comedy series Porridge.

12th | Brian Clough is dismissed after 44 days as manager of defending league champions Leeds United following a disappointing start to the Football League season.

18th | Harold Wilson confirms that a second general election for the year will be held on 10th October.

23rd | Ceefax is started by the BBC – one of the first public service information systems.

26th | Apple Records releases John Lennon's fifth studio album, "Walls & Bridges" in US; features No. 1 single "Whatever Gets You Through the Night" (with Elton John).

October

1st — Five previously all-male Colleges of the University of Oxford admit women undergraduates for the first time.

4th — Apple Records releases John Lennon's fifth studio album, "Walls & Bridges" in UK; features No. 1 single "Whatever Gets You Through the Night".

5th — Guildford pub bombings: Bombs planted by the IRA at pubs patronised by off-duty soldiers, The Horse and Groom and The Seven Stars, kill five people. The bomb in the Horse and Groom, thought to have been planted by a "courting couple" who have never been identified, detonated at 8:30 pm, killing a civilian, two members of the Scots Guards and two members of the Women's Royal Army Corps. The Seven Stars was evacuated after the first blast, and a second bomb exploded at 9:00 pm while the pub landlord and his wife searched the pub. The landlord sustained a fractured skull and his wife a broken leg, and five members of staff and one customer who had just stepped outside received less serious injuries.

10th — The second general election of the year results in a narrow victory for Harold Wilson, giving Labour a majority of three seats. It is widely expected that Edward Heath's leadership of the Conservative Party will soon be at an end, as he has now lost three of the four General Elections that he has contested in almost a decade as leader. The Scottish National Party secures its highest Westminster party representation to date with 11 seats. Enoch Powell is returned to Parliament standing for the Ulster Unionist Party in Northern Ireland. Powell, who was dismissed from the Conservative Shadow Cabinet in April 1968 following his controversial Rivers of Blood speech on immigration, had left the Conservative Party at the general election on 28th February and recently rejected an offer to stand as a candidate for the National Front.

13th — ITV begins airing the American science fiction series Planet of the Apes, based on the successful film franchise and starring Roddy McDowall.

16th — Rioting prisoners set fire to the Maze Prison in Belfast.

The Welsh language soap Pobol y Cwm makes its debut on BBC Wales.

19th — Keith Joseph makes a speech in Edgbaston on the cycle of deprivation; the controversy it provokes has the effect of ruling him out of high office in the Conservative Party.

21st — BBC1 airs the first episode of the children's animated series Roobarb, featuring Roobarb the green dog and Custard the pink cat.

22nd — The IRA bombs Brooks's club in London.

28th — The wife and son of Sports Minister Denis Howell survive an IRA bomb attack on their car.

November

2nd — George Harrison launches his "George Harrison & Friends North American Tour" in Vancouver. It's Harrison's first tour since the Beatles North American Tour of 1966.

4th — Judith Ward is sentenced to life imprisonment for the M62 coach bombing. Her conviction is overturned nearly 18 years later.

November

7th	Lord Lucan disappears after the murder of his children's nanny.
	A Provisional IRA bomb explodes at the Kings Arms, Woolwich.
11th	The New Covent Garden Market in Nine Elms is opened. New Covent Garden Market in Nine Elms, London, is the largest wholesale fruit, vegetable and flower market in the United Kingdom. It covers a site of 57 acres (23 ha) and is home to about 200 fruit, vegetable and flower companies. The market serves 40% of the fruit and vegetables eaten outside of the home in London and provides ingredients to many of London's restaurants, hotels, schools, prisons, hospitals and catering businesses.
13th	McDonald's opens its first UK restaurant in Woolwich, South East London.
21st	Birmingham pub bombings: In Birmingham, England, two pubs are bombed, killing 21 people in an attack widely believed at the time to be linked to the Provisional Irish Republican Army. The Birmingham Six are later sentenced to life in prison for this, but their convictions are quashed after a lengthy campaign.
24th	The Birmingham Six are charged with the Birmingham pub bombings.
25th	Home Secretary Roy Jenkins announces the government's intention to outlaw the IRA in the UK.
27th	The Prevention of Terrorism Act is passed.
28th	John Lennon joins Elton John on stage at Madison Square Garden for three songs. It would be Lennon's last stage performance.

December

5th	"Party Political Broadcast", the final episode of Monty Python's Flying Circus, is broadcast on BBC Two.
6th	George Harrison releases single "Ding Dong, Ding Dong".
15th	New speed limits are introduced on Britain's roads in an attempt to save fuel at a time of Arab fuel embargoes following the Yom Kippur War.

December

18th	The government pays £42,000 to families of victims of Bloody Sunday riots in Northern Ireland. Bloody Sunday, or the Bogside Massacre, was a massacre on 30th January 1972 when British soldiers shot 26 unarmed civilians during a protest march in the Bogside area of Derry, Northern Ireland. Fourteen people died: thirteen were killed outright, while the death of another man four months later was attributed to his injuries. Many of the victims were shot while fleeing from the soldiers, and some were shot while trying to help the wounded. Other protesters were injured by shrapnel, rubber bullets, or batons, two were run down by British Army vehicles, and some were beaten. All of those shot were Catholics. The march had been organised by the Northern Ireland Civil Rights Association (NICRA) to protest against imprisonment without trial. The soldiers were from the 1st Battalion of the Parachute Regiment ("1 Para"), the same battalion implicated in the Ballymurphy massacre several months before.
19th	The ninth James Bond film, The Man with the Golden Gun, premieres in London. It is the second of seven films to star Roger Moore as James Bond.

22nd	The London home of Conservative Party leader and former Prime Minister Edward Heath is bombed in a suspected Provisional IRA attack. He is away from home when the bomb exploded, but returns just 10 minutes afterwards.
24th	Former Cabinet Minister John Stonehouse is found living in Australia having faked his own death in Miami. He is quickly arrested by Australian police, who initially believe that he is Lord Lucan. ITV Anglia exclusively screen the 1966 Batman movie, several years before other regions (ATV Midlands 9 April 1977, Granada and Tyne Tees 29 August 1977 and HTV 29 August 1978).
28th	Tom Baker makes his first full appearance as the Fourth Doctor in the Doctor Who serial Robot.

ADVERTS OF 1974

How the English keep dry for the holidays.

Gordon's Ruddy Merry
Take 1½ oz. of Gordon's Gin, 3 oz. tomato juice, juice of ½ lime, pinch each of salt and pepper, dash of Worcestershire sauce. Shake well with cracked ice.

Gordon's Gin. Largest seller in England, America, the world.

PRODUCT OF U.S.A. 100% NEUTRAL SPIRITS DISTILLED FROM GRAIN. 90 PROOF. GORDON'S DRY GIN CO., LTD., LINDEN, N.J.

15

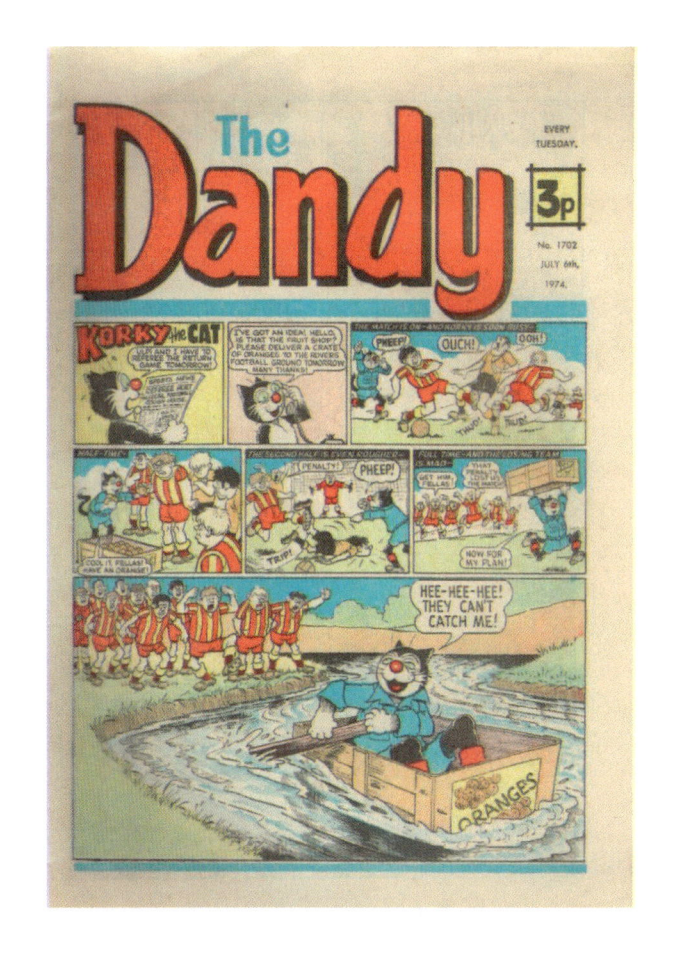

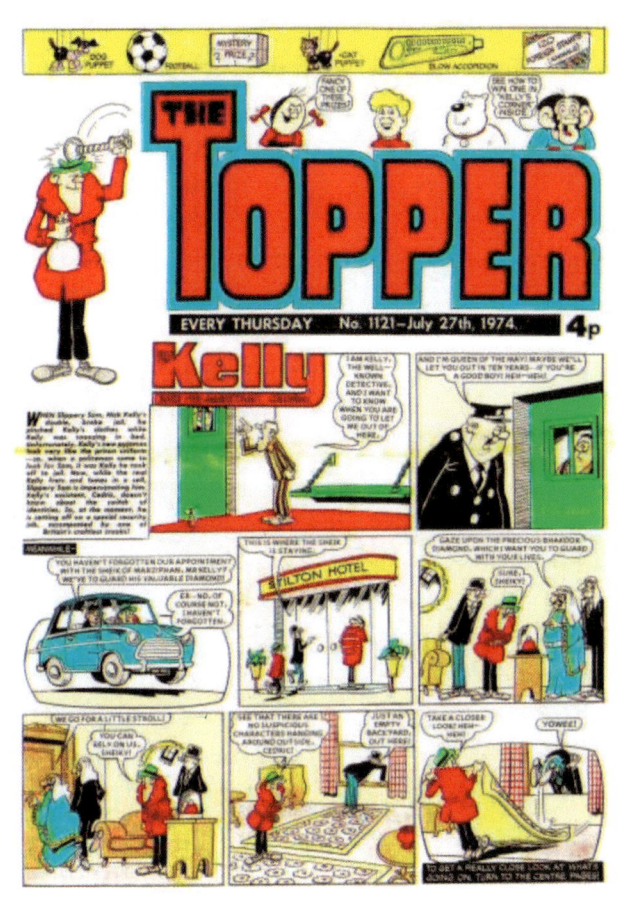

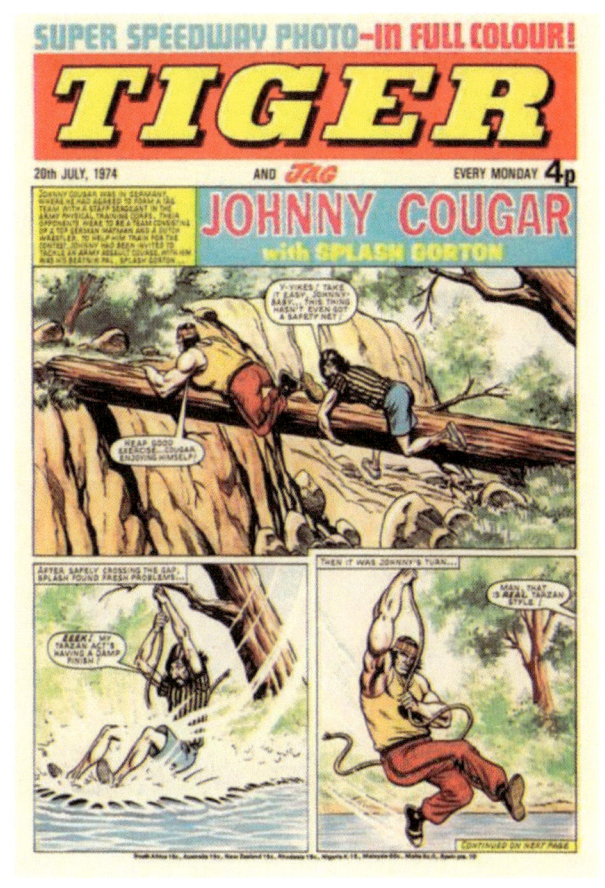

How to make a little petrol go a long way.

Mini

At 60 km/h - 6,1 litres
per 100 kilometres (46 mpg)
At 80 km/h - 7,0 litres
per 100 kilometres (40 mpg)

You can go far.

Apache

At 60 km/h - 5,6 litres
per 100 kilometres (50 mpg)
At 80 km/h - 6,5 litres
per 100 kilometres (43 mpg)

Or even further.

LEYLAND SOUTH AFRICA

Built by Leyland

Technicar February 1974

Petrol consumption figures from Car Magazine Road Tests

AKAI gives you more than just good looks... Now here's the plug:

There's much more to *all* the new AKAI stereo receivers than just great cosmetics. Take a *close* look:

AKAI's new AA-910DB offers outstanding performance at a modest cost. With 24 watts of continuous power at 8 ohms (both channels driven) — enough for most needs. Plus a built-in Dolby® Noise Reduction System. Which means that the AA-910DB provides you with the unique ability to "Dolbyize" any tape or cassette deck used with it.

But maybe you're into 4-channel. Or thinking about it.

Okay! Then check out AKAI's new AS-980 4-channel receiver. 120 watts gives you power to spare. (30W RMS x 4 at 8 ohms — all 4 channels driven.) And a list of exciting features that'll make your eyes pop! Like front panel 2/4 channel switching, 4 individual 4-channel modes — Discrete... SQ ...RM...and CD-4 built-in decoder with individual separation controls, 3 tape monitors with front panel provisions for dubbing, 4 VU meters to assure precise level adjustment for each channel, and an audio muting switch. All just for starters.

So no matter what you're looking for in a quality stereo receiver, look to AKAI...The Innovators.

Then plug it in. And listen.

"Dolby" and "Dolbyize" are Trade Marks of Dolby Laboratories, Inc.

AKAI America, Ltd./Dept. S
2139 E. Del Amo Blvd., Compton,
California 90220

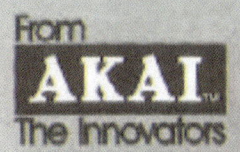

From
AKAI™
The Innovators

People either ask for Beefeater,® or they ask for gin.
IMPORTED FROM ENGLAND
BEEFEATER
LONDON DISTILLED DRY GIN
KOBRAND CORPORATION

Finest English Import since the landing on Plymouth Rock!
EST. 1793
PLYMOUTH
Imported...Coates dry
PLYMOUTH GIN
From Plymouth, England comes Plymouth *Dry* Gin . . . enjoyed for quality in 93 countries . . . famous for the absolutely *dry* Dry Martini (94.4 Proof makes the crackling difference).

BOTTLED IN BOND
OLD FORESTER
It's OLD FORESTER Mint Julep Time Again!
A traditionally famous combination for over 81 years—cool, refreshing mint juleps, made with famous bonded Old Forester! Here is rich, full Kentucky bourbon at its finest. As outstanding for quality and uniformity of flavor as when the first bottle was labeled and signed in the founder's own hand. Truly America's Guest Whisky since 1870!
"There is nothing better in the market"
KENTUCKY STRAIGHT BOURBON WHISKY • BOTTLED IN BOND • 100 PROOF • BROWN-FORMAN DISTILLERS CORPORATION • AT LOUISVILLE IN KENTUCKY

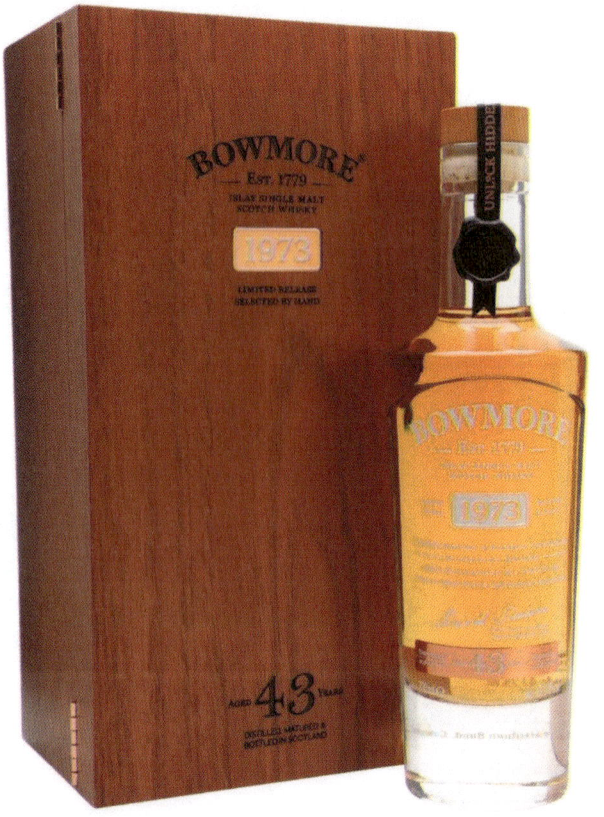
BOWMORE®
Est. 1779
ISLAY SINGLE MALT SCOTCH WHISKY
1973
LIMITED RELEASE
SELECTED BY HAND
AGED 43 YEARS
DISTILLED MATURED & BOTTLED IN SCOTLAND

New Army pay rise!
Now you can start at £17.17*

And... we'll offer you the training you choose.

And... we'll help you see more of the world.

And... we'll give you a varied, exciting life.

And... we'll give you as much sport as you want.

And... we'll make sure you have the best equipment.

The new Army pay scale is now in operation. You should know how much money you'd get, as one of the Professionals.

Men joining on 3-year engagements start at £14.7.

Men on 6-year engagements start at £15.15.

And on 9-year engagements, starting pay is £17.17.

These salaries are fully comparable with civilian pay. The Army charges about £3.13. a week for full board and lodging. You should know the full details. Just fill in the coupon, or call in at your nearest Army Careers Information Office.

*£17.17. is the starting pay for all men who join for nine years.

Join the Professionals

To: Army Careers MP6(A), Lansdowne House, Berkeley Square, London W1X 6AA.
Please send me full details of the new Army pay scale.

NAME
ADDRESS
TOWN   COUNTY
DATE OF BIRTH
M51529704   ARMY

You can't expect great music unless you have great equipment.

In every area of music, a great performance is a rare and beautiful event. In opera, brilliance is achieved when a great score, great vocalists and a great orchestra are brought together. In jazz, greatness is the improvisational genius of musicians performing together.

In your home, greatness means Pioneer. High fidelity equipment that delivers truly superior performance. Performance that can only be achieved when excellence is your standard and innovation is your way of life.

For truly great performance, choose your music system from the complete line of Pioneer audio components. Great music is a rare and beautiful event — with great equipment from Pioneer.

PIONEER when you want something better

U.S. Pioneer Electronics Corp.
75 Oxford Drive, Moonachie, New Jersey 07074 / West: 13300 S. Estrella, Los Angeles 90248 / Midwest: 1500 Greenleaf, Elk Grove Village, Ill. 60007 / Canada: S. H. Parker Co.

How to make a little petrol go a long way.

Mini
At 60 km/h - 6,1 litres per 100 kilometres (46 mpg)
At 80 km/h - 7,0 litres per 100 kilometres (40 mpg)
You can go far.

Apache
At 60 km/h - 5,6 litres per 100 kilometres (50 mpg)
At 80 km/h - 6,5 litres per 100 kilometres (43 mpg)
Or even further.

LEYLAND SOUTH AFRICA
Built by Leyland

Petrol consumption figures from Car Magazine Road Tests

TVTimes 8p
MY LIFE WITH ILIE by MRS. NASTY see page 8
ATV Midlands NOV 9-15
EAMONN ANDREWS returns with THIS IS YOUR LIFE on Wednesday

DAF

—HERE'S JUST A SAMPLE OF OUR FINE RANGE OF USED CARS ...
New DAF 66 SL Estate. Finished in Torrana ... £1,530
New DAF 66 SL Saloon. Finished in Kobina ... £1,430
New DAF 66 Marathon 1100 Coupe. Finished in Kobina/black ... £1,498
1974 DAF 66 SL Marathon, Averto/black ... £1,395
1974 DAF 66 SL 1300, Terrana/black ... £1,250
1974 DAF 44 Saloon, only 1,000 miles ... £1,095
1973 DAF 33. 12,000 miles. Toendra/black ... £775
1973 DAF 66 SL Coupe, marina/black £1,195
1972 DAF 44 Saloon, red/black ... £745
1972 DAF 33 Saloon, green/beige £665
1969 DAF 33 Saloon, green/beige £395
1970 MORRIS 1300, Auto., low mileage ... £625

THE DAF CENTRE
NORTHAMPTON HOUSE, CHARLES STREET, LEIC. Tel. 56281.
Works and Stores:
PIKE STREET, LEICESTER Tel. 21007/8.

DAF Authorised Dealer

For the gardener who has everything—except a gardener!

If you've a large garden or a small estate and you cannot get a gardener for love nor money–take a good look at the John Deere range of all-year-round Estate Tractors and Ride-on Mowers. They're ruggedly made–on the same lines as full size agricultural machines. Yet they're beautifully designed, compact, incredibly easy to handle and a joy to own and operate. The larger models incorporate the advanced hydrostatic drive, and with a big range of ancillary equipment–rotary cultivators, dump trucks, etc–they do far more than cut the grass.

In fact, once you've used a John Deere Estate Tractor or Ride-on Mower, you'll wonder how you ever managed without! Send for full colour brochures, and the name and address of your nearest Stanhay distributor–(these are exclusive machines–you can't buy them just anywhere).

Please send me literature on the John Deere range, and the name and address of my nearest distributor.

Name..............
Address..............

TO: Bob Haldin, Stanhay (Ashford) Limited, Godinton Works, Ashford, Kent.

BUY BRITISH! BUY BEST! BUY NOW!

BRITAIN'S GREATEST MOTOR SHOW OFFER!
ON 50 NEW MINIS FROM STOCK

SAVE £82 WE PAY YOUR VAT AMOUNT

OFFER ONLY VALID ON PRODUCTION OF THIS ADVERT

MARINAS
1.3, 1.8 COUPE AND SALOONS, ESTATES AND VANS
CHOOSE FROM 40
★ SAVE UP TO £100

ALLEGROS
1100, 1300, 1500, 1750 MANUALS AND AUTOMATICS.
CHOOSE FROM 30
★ SAVE UP TO £175

PART EXCHANGE WELCOME
LEYLAND'S GREATEST ACHIEVEMENT

★ SIMILAR TERMS ON ALL OTHER MODELS OF AUSTIN - MORRIS - MG ★

BRITISH LEYLAND

BARKINGSIDE MOTOR CO
FENCEPIECE RD., BARKINGSIDE, ESSEX.
01-500 0911.

NEW CROWN MOTORS
RAINHAM RD. SOUTH, DAGENHAM, ESSEX.
01-592 0991.

COST OF LIVING 1974

A conversion of pre-decimal to decimal money

The Pound, 1971 became the year of decimalization when the pound became 100 new pennies. Prior to that the pound was equivalent to 20 shillings. Money prior to 1971 was written £/s/d. (d being for pence). Below is a chart explaining the monetary value of each coin before and after 1971.

Symbol	Before 1971	After 1971
£	Pound (240 pennies)	Pound (100 new pennies)
s	Shilling (12 pennies)	5 pence
d	Penny	¼ of a penny
¼d	Farthing	1 penny
½d	Halfpenny	½ pence
3d	Threepence	About 1/80 of a pound
4d	Groat (four pennies)	
6d	Sixpence (Tanner)	2½ new pence
2s	Florin (2 shillings)	10 pence
2s/6d	Half a crown (2 shillings and 6 pence)	12½ pence
5s	Crown	25 pence
10s	10 shilling note (10 bob)	50 pence
10s/6d	½ Guinea	52½ pence
21s	1 Guinea	105 pence

Prices are in equivalent to new pence today and on average throughout the UK.

Item	1974	Price equivalent today
Average house price	£10,000.00	£180,000.00
Ford Cortina	£1,519.00	£19.000
Gallon of petrol	£0.50p	£4.00

Full-time manual worker - male (aged 21 and over) £48.63
Full-time manual worker - female (aged 18 and over) £27.01
Sailor in the Royal Navy - £26 per week at age 18
Traffic warden - £28.50 per week
International telephonist (male) - £28.50 per week
Typist at the Department of Trade and Industry (London) - £26.05-£28.05 per week
Double glazing salesman (Alpine Double Glazing) - up to £11,000 pa
Coach trimmer and finisher at Leyland cars - £67.30 per week
Production worker at Ford - £60.50 per week
London bus driver - £38.50 per week (including overtime)

	Prices in 1974	Price with inflation
Bottle of whisky (Haig) (Co-op)	**£2.57**	**£21.00**
Bottle of sherry (Harvey's Bristol Cream) (Co-op)	£1.69	£14.00
Watney's Party 4 (Co-op)	**60p**	**£4.80**
Watney's Party 7 (Mac Markets)	£1.00	£8.00
Pint of Beer	22½p	£1.80
Pint of Milk	4½p	36p
Large loaf of bread	14½p	£1.20
½lb Emblem butter (Tesco)	10½p	85p
Nescafé 8oz coffee (Tesco)	69p	£5.50
Can of Coke (Tesco)	7½p	60p
The Daily Mirror newspaper	3-5p	24-40p
Golden Wonder crisps	**7p**	**56p**
One dozen large white eggs	45p	£3.60
Bendix Auto washer Deluxe automatic washing machine (Currys)	£110.00	£890.00
Hotpoint Supermatic twin tub washing machine (Currys)	£74.95	£600.00
Zoppas Fridge-Freezer (Currys)	**£104.95**	**£840.00**

Pools wins

Britain's record pools win in 1974 was £680,697. Allowing for inflation that would be worth £5 million today.

The 70s keg beer and lager
At the beginning of the 70s, the most popular brands of keg bitter dominated British beer drinking. They were more expensive than cask bitters, so people must have liked the taste or bought the advertising.

Advertising of keg bitters made extravagant claims. Whitbread Tankard was supposed to help you excel, how, was not made clear. Beer had long been advertised as a drink to improve heath. The "Guinness is Good for You" and "Guinness for Strength" campaigns are famous. Was a touch of parody intended?

Rivals made equally bold claims. Worthington 'E' was "the taste that satisfies". Courage Tavern was "What your right arm's for". Double Diamond "worked wonders".

Raleigh Chopper 5 1972-1976
he Raleigh Chopper 5 had a new gear change based on the classic racing bike derailleur, but with the Chopper style gear shift.

Strangely, it was only available in pink, a colour guaranteed not to appeal to boys in the 1970s. The Raleigh brochure called this 'Sharp Pink'. It also had red and yellow lettering.

Like the Sprint, it did not sell well and was quietly dropped in 1976.

It is, of course, highly collectable today. Expect to pay around £1000 for a good one.

On the 26th November 2008, trading of shares in Woolworths Group was suspended, and its Woolworths and Entertainment UK subsidiaries entered administration. Deloitte closed all 807 Woolworth's stores between the 27th December 2008 and the 6th January 2009, resulting in 27,000 job losses. Woolworths Group plc entered administration on 27th January 2009, and it was officially dissolved on the 13th October 2015.

In February 2009, Shop Direct Group purchased the Woolworths trademark and internet address, which continued as a retail website until its closure in June 2015. As of April 2017, after former director Tony Page expressed a wish to buy the Woolworths name from Shop Direct, there was talk of Woolworths making a comeback to British high streets.

BRITISH BIRTHS

Melanie Jayne Chisholm was born on 12th January 1974 and is professionally known as Melanie C or Mel C, is an English singer-songwriter, DJ, businesswoman and media personality. As one of the five members of the Spice Girls, she was nicknamed Sporty Spice. She rose to fame in 1996 with the Spice Girls, with whom she released two consecutive number-one albums and eight number-one singles. Chisholm has co-written 11 UK number-ones, more than any other female artist in chart history. In October 2009, she had her acting debut on stage as Mrs Johnstone in the musical Blood Brothers. In 2015, Chisholm joined the judging panel for Asia's Got Talent, along with David Foster, Anggun Cipta, and Vanness Wu. They started the selection in Singapore. During production and selections, Chisholm lived in Malaysia, where the program was recorded. In February 2022, Chisholm appeared as a guest judge on the first episode of RuPaul's Drag Race: UK Versus the World. Melanie has cited Madonna as her biggest musical influence.

Sarah Caroline Sinclair CBE (née Colman); was born 30th January 1974. She is known professionally as Olivia Colman and is an English actress. Known for her work in film and television. Colman received the BAFTA Award for Best Female Comedy Performance for the comedy programme Twenty Twelve (2011–2012) and Best Supporting Actress for the crime programme Accused (2012). She was acclaimed for her performance in the ITV crime-drama series Broadchurch (2013–2017), for which she received a British Academy Television Award for Best Actress. Colman also appeared in the BBC One thriller miniseries The Night Manager (2016), for which she received a Golden Globe Award for Best Supporting Actress. Colman starred with Anthony Hopkins in Florian Zeller's 2020 film adaptation of his stage play, The Father, which focuses on an elderly man dealing with memory loss. Olivia Colman will appear in the musical film Wonka, which explores Willy Wonka's origins as a prequel to the Roald Dahl novel Charlie and the Chocolate Factory.

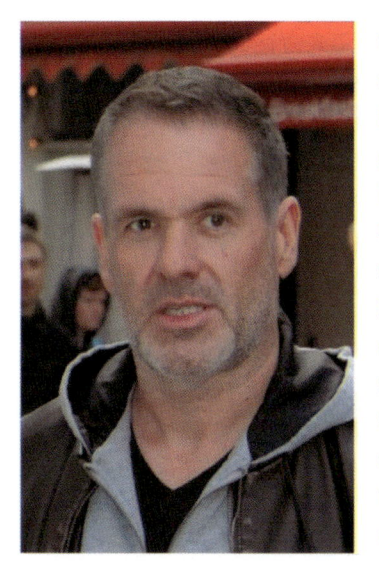

Christopher David Moyles was born 22nd February 1974 and is an English radio and television presenter, author and presenter of The Chris Moyles Show on Radio X. On 5th January 2004, Moyles started presenting Radio 1's breakfast programme, named The Chris Moyles Show, switching places with Sara Cox. He had been appointed to increase the ratings for the show and did so, putting on an extra 1,000,000 listeners to the audience in the first quarter of 2004. After a successful first year, Moyles was awarded 'DJ of the Year' by readers of The Sun. On 7 September 2015, it was announced Chris Moyles would return to radio on the newly re-branded Radio X hosting the new Chris Moyles Show. The show began airing on 21st September 2015 from 6.30 am–10.00 am. On 31st October 2022 Moyles was announced by ITV as a campmate of the 2022 series of I'm a Celebrity...Get Me Out of Here! In 2012 Chris Moyles was involved in a tax avoidance scheme and requested a court order to prevent the press from reporting it, because he claimed it would infringe his human rights.

Zöe Elizabeth Lucker was born on born 11th April 1974 and is an English actress. In 2002, Lucker began portraying the role of Tanya Turner on ITV drama series, Footballers' Wives. In 2004, she was nominated and won a TV Quick and TV Choice Award for Best Actress for her role of Tanya Turner; she was also nominated for a National Television Award in the category of Most Popular Actress for her work on Footballers' Wives. She also appeared in BBC drama series, HolbyBlue, playing the role of Kate Keenan. In 2009, Lucker appeared on Who Wants to Be a Millionaire? alongside John Suchet, winning £150,000 for the Caron Keating Foundation. In March 2010, Lucker joined the cast of BBC soap opera, EastEnders, to portray the role Vanessa Gold. She left in October 2011. In February 2015, Lucker joined the cast of Hollyoaks, to play Reenie McQueen. She made her first appearance on 16 April 2015. It was later announced in December 2015 that Lucker would be leaving the role at the conclusion of the child sexual abuse storyline.

Victoria Caroline Beckham OBE was born on 17th April 1974 is an English fashion designer, singer, and television personality. She rose to prominence in the 1990s as a member of the girl group the Spice Girls, in which she was nicknamed Posh Spice. With over 100 million records sold worldwide. The group became the best-selling female group of all time. After the Spice Girls split in 2001, Beckham was signed to Virgin Records, in which she released her self-titled debut solo album, which produced two UK Top 10 singles. Beckham has become an internationally recognised style icon and fashion designer. Following high-profile collaborations with other brands, she launched an eponymous label in 2008, and a lower-priced (diffusion) label in 2011. The Victoria Beckham label was named designer brand of the year in the UK in 2011. Victoria was appointed an OBE in the 2017 New Year Honours for services to the fashion industry. She is married to former association football player David Beckham, and they have four children, including Brooklyn. As of May 2019, the couple's joint wealth is estimated at £355 million.

Vernon Charles Kay was born 28th April 1974 is an English television and radio presenter, and former model. He presented Channel 4's T4 (2000–2005) and has presented various television shows for ITV, including All Star Family Fortunes (2006–2015), Just the Two of Us (2006–2007), Beat the Star (2008–2009), The Whole 19 Yards (2010), Splash! (2013–2014), and 1000 Heartbeats (2015–2016). Kay presented his own BBC Radio 1 show between 2004 and 2012, and presented his own show on Radio X between 2015 and 2017. Since the start of the 2018–19 season, he has been the main presenter for the live coverage of Formula E for English speaking territories/platforms around the world. In 2023, Kay was announced as the new mid-morning host on BBC Radio 2 from May 2023, taking over the slot from Ken Bruce, who had left the previous month to join Greatest Hits Radio. In 2020, Kay appeared on the twentieth series of I'm a Celebrity...Get Me Out of Here! finishing in third place, behind Jordan North and the eventual Queen of the Castle, Giovanna Fletcher.

Denise van Outen was born 27th May 1974 and is an English actress, singer, dancer and presenter. As a teenager, van Outen had brief roles on a number of television dramas; these included Kappatoo and The Bill. In 1992, she appeared in a Drinking and Driving Wrecks Lives commercial. During her first stint on The Big Breakfast show, she appeared as Jill in ITV1's version of the pantomime Jack and the Beanstalk alongside Julie Walters and Neil Morrissey. Wanting to further develop her acting career, she left The Big Breakfast at the end of 1998. In February 2015, it was announced that Van Outen would be joining the cast of EastEnders. Van Outen plays intelligent businesswoman Karin Smart who gets involved with Max Branning (Jake Wood). In September 2012, van Outen was announced as one of the celebrities competing on the tenth series of Strictly Come Dancing. She partnered with professional dancer James Jordan. On 23 September 2020, van Outen was announced as one of the celebrities competing on the thirteenth series of Dancing on Ice. She was partnered with Matt Evers.

David James Stuart Mitchell was born 14th July 1974 and is a British comedian, actor, writer and television personality. He is part of the comedy duo Mitchell and Webb, alongside Robert Webb. Mitchell and Webb starred in the Channel 4 sitcom Peep Show, in which Mitchell plays Mark Corrigan. Mitchell won the British Academy Television Award for Best Comedy Performance in 2009 for his performance. The duo has written and starred in several sketch shows including Bruiser, The Mitchell and Webb Situation, That Mitchell and Webb Sound and also That Mitchell and Webb Look. The pair also starred in the UK version of Apple's "Get a Mac" advertising campaign. In 2013, the duo starred in the short-lived TV series Ambassadors. Since 2017, Mitchell has starred in the Channel 4 comedy-drama Back, alongside Webb. Mitchell is a frequent participant on British panel shows, being a team captain on Would I Lie to You? and the host of The Unbelievable Truth on BBC Radio 4. As a writer, Mitchell contributes comment articles to the British newspapers The Observer and The Guardian.

Emilia Rose Elizabeth Fox was born 31 July 1974 and is an English actress and presenter. Fox first appeared as Georgiana, the sister of Colin Firth's Mr. Darcy, in the 1995 television adaptation of Pride and Prejudice. In 2004, she joined the cast of the crime drama, Silent Witness. As of 2023, she is still in the show and has now played the role of Nikki Alexander for nineteen years. in 2007, Fox was reunited with her Rebecca co-star Charles Dance when they starred together in the ITV1 mini-series Fallen Angel, Fox played a serial killer Rosie Byfield, with Dance appearing as her father. She narrated the Doctor Who character Lady Winters in the Doctor Who Adventure Game, The Gunpowder Plot, (2011). She had previously played Berenice in the Eighth Doctor audio drama Nevermore. In 2015, she appeared as Julia Swetlove in the BBC's dramatization of J. K. Rowling's book The Casual Vacancy. The following year, she appeared in series 2 of The Tunnel as Vanessa Hamilton. In 2016–18 she starred as Sam Vincent in Delicious, a Sky television drama.

Louise Elizabeth Redknapp was born 4th November 1974 and known as Louise, is an English singer and media personality. She was a member of Eternal, an R&B girl group which debuted in 1993 with their quadruple-platinum studio album Always & Forever. In 1995, she departed from the group for a solo career. At the start of 1998, Redknapp's career was at a high point: her second album had gone platinum, she was on the cover of magazines such as Smash Hits and GQ, and she had been voted Sexiest Woman in the World by the readers of FHM magazine. In 2002, Redknapp signed a £1.5 million contract with her manager Oliver Smallman's Positive Records (a division of Universal Music) to record her fourth solo album. The album was due for release in 2004 alongside the single "Bounce Back". However, due to the singer becoming pregnant with her son Charley, the album was never released. In May 2021, Redknapp appeared on The Masked Dancer masked as Flamingo. She was the second celebrity to be unmasked.

Benjamin Peter Sherrington Shephard was born 11th December 1974 and is an English television presenter and journalist who is currently employed by ITV. Shephard's career took off in 1998, when he began hosting Channel 4 spin-off show The Bigger Breakfast, alongside fellow presenters including Josie D'Arby, Melanie Sykes and Dermot O'Leary. That same year, Shephard became the first presenter of T4's teen strand on Channel 4, which launched on 25th October 1998. Between 2005 and 2011, Shephard was a stand-in presenter on This Morning, covering for regular presenter Phillip Schofield. Shephard has presented the popular daytime game show Tipping Point since 2012, as well as celebrity episodes known as Tipping Point: Lucky Stars since 2013. In June 2015, it was announced that Tipping Point had been renewed for two further series to air in 2016 and 2017. After just four years on air, Daybreak was axed in spring 2014 to make way for a brand new ITV Breakfast programme Good Morning Britain.

Sara Joanne Cyzer (nee Cox) was born 13th December 1974 is an English broadcaster. Cox won her first television show role in 1996, presenting the early "Girl Power" show The Girlie Show on Channel 4. She later had stints on Channel 5 entertainment show Exclusive and Channel 4 music programme Born Sloppy. In September 1998, Cox became a presenter of The Big Breakfast, following in the footsteps of her close friend Zoe Ball. A transfer to radio came on 19 September 1999 when she joined BBC Radio 1. She launched the hugely popular The Surgery with Mark Hamilton, where Cox acted as "Nurse Coxy". In December 1999, it was announced that Cox would again step into Zoe Ball's shoes as presenter of Radio 1 Breakfast. Cox's breakfast show stint began on 3 April 2000. Initially, her listening figures were very good, growing from 6.9 million to 7.8 million listeners during her first fifteen months in the job—earning Radio 1 its largest breakfast audience ever. In October 2020, Cox launched and presented Between the Covers on BBC Two, a seven-episode book programme, renewing for five series, as of December 2022.

BRITISH DEATHS

Herbert Ernest Bates CBE born 16th May 1905 and passed away 29th January 1974. He was better known as H. E. Bates and was an English writer. Typically, Bates' best-known works are set in the English countryside, particularly the Midlands including his native Northamptonshire and the 'Garden of England', Kent, the setting for The Darling Buds of May. Bates was partial to taking long walks around the Northamptonshire countryside and this often provided the inspiration for his stories. During World War II, he was commissioned into the Royal Air Force solely to write short stories. The Air Ministry realised that it might create more favourable public sentiment by emphasizing stories about the people fighting the war, rather than facts. His most popular creation was the Larkin family in The Darling Buds of May. Pop Larkin and his family were inspired by a person seen in a local shop in Kent by Bates and his family when on holiday. The television adaptation, produced after his death by his son Richard and based on these stories.

Prince Henry, Duke of Gloucester (Henry William Frederick Albert) was born 31st March 1900 and died 10th June 1974. He was the third son and fourth child of King George V and Queen Mary. Henry was the first son of a British monarch to be educated at school, where he excelled at sports, and went on to attend Eton College, after which he was commissioned in the 10th Royal Hussars, a regiment he hoped to command. From 1939 to 1940, Henry served in France as a liaison officer to Lord Gort. He performed military and diplomatic duties during the rest of the war, then in 1945 was appointed as Australia's governor-general. The post had originally been offered to his younger brother the Duke of Kent, who died in an air crash. Henry attended the coronation of his niece Queen Elizabeth II in 1953 and carried out several overseas tours, often accompanied by his wife. Upon his death, he was succeeded as the Duke of Gloucester by his only living son, Richard.

Sir James Chadwick, CH, FRS was born 20th October 1891 and died 24th July 1974. He was a British physicist who was awarded the 1935 Nobel Prize in Physics for his discovery of the neutron in 1932. Chadwick graduated from the Victoria University of Manchester in 1911, where he studied under Ernest Rutherford. During the Second World War, Chadwick carried out research as part of the Tube Alloys project to build an atom bomb, while his Manchester lab and environs were harassed by Luftwaffe bombing. Shortly after the war ended, Chadwick was appointed to the Advisory Committee on Atomic Energy (ACAE). He was also appointed as the British scientific advisor to the United Nations Atomic Energy Commission. He clashed with fellow ACAE member Patrick Blackett, who disagreed with Chadwick's conviction that Britain needed to acquire its own nuclear weapons; but it was Chadwick's position that was ultimately adopted. He returned to Britain in 1946, to find a country still beset by wartime rationing and shortages.

SPORTING EVENTS 1974

1974 County Cricket Season

The 1974 County Championship was the 75th officially organised running of the County Championship. Worcestershire won the Championship title. Worcestershire County Cricket Club is one of eighteen first-class county clubs within the domestic cricket structure of England and Wales. It represents the historic county of Worcestershire. Its Vitality Blast T20 team has been rebranded the Worcestershire Rapids, but the county is known by most fans as 'the Pears'. The club is based at New Road, Worcester. Founded in 1865, Worcestershire held minor status at first and was a prominent member of the early Minor Counties Championship in the 1890s, winning the competition three times. In 1899, the club joined the County Championship and the team was elevated to first-class status. Since then, Worcestershire have played in every top-level domestic cricket competition in England.

County Championship table

Team	Pld	Won	Lost	Drawn	Tie	Batting bonus	Bowling bonus	Points
Worcestershire	20	11	3	6	0	45	72	227
Hampshire	19	10	3	6	0	55	70	225
Northamptonshire	20	9	2	9	0	46	67	203
Leicestershire	20	7	7	6	0	47	69	186
Somerset	20	6	4	10	0	49	72	181
Middlesex	20	7	5	8	0	45	56	171
Surrey	20	6	4	10	0	42	69	171
Lancashire	20	5	0	15	0	47	66	163
Warwickshire	20	5	5	10	0	44	65	159
Kent	20	5	8	7	0	33	63	146
Yorkshire	19	4	7	8	0	37	69	146
Essex	20	4	3	12	1	44	52	146
Sussex	20	4	9	6	1	29	63	141
Gloucestershire	19	4	9	6	0	29	55	124
Nottinghamshire	20	1	9	10	0	42	66	118
Glamorgan	19	2	7	10	0	28	56	104
Derbyshire	20	1	6	13	0	23	62	95

1973–74 in English football

Don Revie marked his last season as Leeds United's manager by guiding them to the league championship, before taking over from Sir Alf Ramsey as the England national team manager, with England having failed to qualify for the 1974 World Cup. Revie's Leeds side beat Liverpool to the title by five points to win it for the second time in their history. Despite the sensational dismissal of manager Brian Clough only 18 months after he won the First Division with the club, Derby County regrouped well under new manager Dave Mackay to finish third and qualify for the UEFA Cup, along with Ipswich Town and Stoke City. Newly promoted Burnley finished in sixth place.

Pos	Team	Pld	W	D	L	GF	GA	GR	Pts	Qualification or relegation
1	Leeds United	42	24	14	4	66	31	2.129	62	Qualified for the European Cup
2	Liverpool	42	22	13	7	52	31	1.677	57	Qualified for the Cup Winners' Cup
3	Derby County	42	17	14	11	52	42	1.238	48	Qualified for the UEFA Cup[a]
4	Ipswich Town	42	18	11	13	67	58	1.155	47	
5	Stoke City	42	15	16	11	54	42	1.286	46	
6	Burnley	42	16	14	12	56	53	1.057	46	
7	Everton	42	16	12	14	50	48	1.042	44	
8	Queens Park Rangers	42	13	17	12	56	52	1.077	43	
9	Leicester City	42	13	16	13	51	41	1.244	42	
10	Arsenal	42	14	14	14	49	51	0.961	42	
11	Tottenham Hotspur	42	14	14	14	45	50	0.900	42	
12	Wolverhampton Wanderers	42	13	15	14	49	49	1.000	41	Qualified for the UEFA Cup[a]
13	Sheffield United	42	14	12	16	44	49	0.898	40	
14	Manchester City	42	14	12	16	39	46	0.848	40	
15	Newcastle United	42	13	12	17	49	48	1.021	38	
16	Coventry City	42	14	10	18	43	54	0.796	38	
17	Chelsea	42	12	13	17	56	60	0.933	37	
18	West Ham United	42	11	15	16	55	60	0.917	37	
19	Birmingham City	42	12	13	17	52	64	0.813	37	
20	Southampton	42	11	14	17	47	68	0.691	36	Relegated to the Second Division
21	Manchester United	42	10	12	20	38	48	0.792	32	
22	Norwich City	42	7	15	20	37	62	0.597	29	

1973–74 Scottish Division One

The 1973–74 Scottish Division One was won by Celtic by four points over nearest rival Hibernian. East Fife and Falkirk finished 17th and 18th respectively and were relegated to the 1974–75 Second Division. This was Celtic's ninth title in a row, a record that would be equalled by Rangers in the 1996–97 season and again by Celtic themselves in 2019–20. The club has won the Scottish league championship 51 times, most recently in 2019–20, the Scottish Cup 40 times and the Scottish League Cup 20 times. The club's greatest season was 1966–67, when Celtic became the first British team to win the European Cup, also winning the Scottish league championship, the Scottish Cup, the League Cup and the Glasgow Cup. Celtic also reached the 1970 European Cup Final and the 2003 UEFA Cup Final, losing in both. Celtic have a long-standing fierce rivalry with Rangers, and the clubs are known as the Old Firm, seen by some as the world's biggest football derby.

Division 1

Pos	Team	Pld	W	D	L	GF	GA	GD	Pts	Qualification or relegation
1	Celtic	34	23	7	4	82	27	+55	53	Champion
2	Hibernian	34	20	9	5	75	42	+33	49	
3	Rangers	34	21	6	7	67	34	+33	48	
4	Aberdeen	34	13	16	5	46	26	+20	42	
5	Dundee	34	16	7	11	67	48	+19	39	
6	Heart of Midlothian	34	14	10	10	54	43	+11	38	
7	Ayr United	34	15	8	11	44	40	+4	38	
8	Dundee United	34	15	7	12	55	51	+4	37	1974–75 European Cup Winners' Cup First round
9	Motherwell	34	14	7	13	45	40	+5	35	
10	Dumbarton	34	11	7	16	43	58	−15	29	
11	Partick Thistle	34	9	10	15	33	46	−13	28	
12	St Johnstone	34	9	10	15	41	60	−19	28	
13	Arbroath	34	10	7	17	52	69	−17	27	
14	Morton	34	8	10	16	37	49	−12	26	
15	Clyde	34	8	9	17	29	65	−36	25	
16	Dunfermline Athletic	34	8	8	18	43	65	−22	24	
17	East Fife	34	9	6	19	26	51	−25	24	Relegated to 1974–75 Second Division
18	Falkirk	34	4	14	16	33	58	−25	22	

1974 Five Nations Championship

The 1974 Five Nations Championship was the forty-fifth series of the rugby union Five Nations Championship. Including the previous incarnations as the Home Nations and Five Nations, this was the eightieth series of the northern hemisphere rugby union championship. Ten matches were played between 19 January and 16 March. It was contested by England, France, Ireland, Scotland and Wales. The championship was won by Ireland, the team's eighth outright title (seven other titles had been shared with other teams).

This was the first time ever that two games were played on the same weekend. This was brought in after the request from some teams, who complained that they had to always play early on in the year when bad weather prevailed, but others played in March, when the weather was better.

To get around this problem, the new format saw each team play each other's fixtures in a rotational period of scheduling. As an example, Scotland played England last in 1975, 1980, 1985. In 1976, 1981, 1986, 1991, the Scotland v England fixture was on the second weekend.

The 1974 tournament was closely contested with three of the matches ending in draws. Ireland topped the table after four rounds but had to sit out the final round of matches. Both France and Wales had chances to win the title, but both lost their last games. Welsh winger J. J. Williams appeared to score a winning try late in their game against England, but it was disallowed by referee John West, an Irishman, leading singer and Welsh rugby fan Max Boyce to compose a song about "blind Irish referees".

Teams

Nation	Venue	City	Head coach	Captain
England	Twickenham	London	John Elders	John Pullin
France	Parc des Princes	Paris	Jean Desclaux	Max Barrau/Elie Cester
Ireland	Lansdowne Road	Dublin	Syd Millar	Willie John McBride
Scotland	Murrayfield	Edinburgh	Bill Dickinson	Ian McLauchlan
Wales	National Stadium	Cardiff	Clive Rowlands	Gareth Edwards

Table

Position	Nation	Played	Won	Drawn	Lost	For	Against	Difference	Table points
1	Ireland	4	2	1	1	50	45	+5	5
2	Scotland	4	2	0	2	41	35	+6	4
2	Wales	4	1	2	1	43	41	+2	4
2	France	4	1	2	1	43	53	−10	4
5	England	4	1	1	2	63	66	−3	3

The Open 1974

The 1974 Open Championship was the 103rd Open Championship, held from 10–13 July at Royal Lytham & St Annes Golf Club in Lancashire, England. Gary Player won his third Open Championship, four strokes ahead of runner-up Peter Oosterhuis. It was the eighth of his nine major titles and second of the year; he won the Masters in April. In the other two majors in 1974, the U.S. Open and the PGA Championship, Player had top ten finishes.

Player is one of the most successful golfers in history, tied for fourth in major championship victories with nine. Along with Arnold Palmer and Jack Nicklaus he is often referred to as one of "The Big Three" golfers of his era – from the late 1950s through the late 1970s – when golf boomed in the United States and around the world and was greatly encouraged by expanded television coverage. Along with Gene Sarazen, Ben Hogan, Jack Nicklaus, and Tiger Woods, he is one of only five players to win golf's "career Grand Slam". He completed the Grand Slam in 1965 at the age of twenty-nine. Player was the second multiple majors' winner from South Africa, following Bobby Locke, then was followed by Ernie Els, and Retief Goosen.

Place	Player	Score	To par	Money (£)
1	Gary Player	69-68-75-70=282	−2	5,500
2	Peter Oosterhuis	71-71-73-71=286	+2	4,000
3	Jack Nicklaus	74-72-70-71=287	+3	3,250
4	Hubert Green	71-74-72-71=288	+4	2,750
T5	Danny Edwards	70-73-76-73=292	+8	2,300
T5	Lu Liang-Huan	72-72-75-73=292	+8	2,300
T7	Bobby Cole	70-72-76-75=293	+9	1,717
T7	Donald Swaelens	77-73-74-69=293	+9	1,717
T7	Tom Weiskopf	72-72-74-75=293	+9	1,717
10	Johnny Miller	72-75-73-74=294	+10	1,500

Nicknamed the Black Knight, Mr. Fitness, and the International Ambassador of Golf, he is also a renowned golf course architect with more than 400 design projects on five continents throughout the world. Player has also authored or co-written 36 books on golf instruction, design, philosophy, motivation and fitness. On 7th January 2021, Player was awarded the Presidential Medal of Freedom by United States President Donald Trump.

The Player Group operates The Player Foundation, which has a primary objective of promoting underprivileged education around the world. In 1983, The Player Foundation established the Blair Atholl Schools in Johannesburg, South Africa, which has educational facilities for more than 500 students from kindergarten through eighth grade. In 2013 it celebrated its 30th anniversary with charity golf events in London, Palm Beach, Shanghai and Cape Town, bringing its total of funds raised to over US$60 million.

Grand National 1974

The 1974 Grand National was the 128th renewal of the Grand National horse race that took place at Aintree near Liverpool, England, on 30 March 1974. The race is famous for the second of Red Rum's three Grand National wins. L'Escargot finished second. Red Rum retained his title at the 1974 National, carrying 12 stone. (He followed that with victory in the Scottish Grand National, and remains the only horse to win both in the same season.) Red Rum came second in 1975 and 1976; Tommy Stack replaced Fletcher as jockey in the 1976 race after Fletcher angered trainer Ginger McCain by telling the press the horse no longer felt right after a defeat in a race away from Aintree. Again, Red Rum saved his best for Aintree but was held off by Rag Trade. The following year, Stack rode the 12-year-old Red Rum to his record third Grand National triumph, in what is regarded as one of the greatest moments in horse racing history.

Position	Name	Jockey	Age	Handicap (st-lb)	SP
01	Red Rum	Brian Fletcher	9	12-0	11/1
02	L'Escargot	Tommy Carberry	11	11-13	17/2
03	Charles Dickens	Andy Turnell	10	10-0	50/1

2,000 Guineas 1974

Nonoalco, trained by François Boutin, had an outstanding year in racing. He won the Prix Yacowlef, Prix Morny and the Prix de la Salamandre, plus he finished second in the Grand Critérium to Nelson Bunker Hunt's colt, Mississipian. As a three-year-old, he won the British Classic, the 2000 Guineas in 1974 at Newmarket Racecourse, beating the odds-on favourite Apalachee into third place. In France, he captured the Prix du Rond Point and the Prix Jacques Le Marois.

St Leger 1974

Bustino was a British Thoroughbred racehorse and sire. In a career which lasted from August 1973 until July 1975, he ran nine times and won five races. As a three-year-old in 1974, the colt began by winning the Sandown Classic Trial from the future Epsom Derby winner Snow Knight, who was carrying five pounds more in weight. In the Lingfield Derby Trial he again defeated Snow Knight, this time at level weights. At Epsom, he seemed to be unsuited by the firm ground and finished fourth in the Derby, behind Snow Knight, Imperial Prince and Giacometti. Bustino was then sent to France for the Grand Prix de Paris at Longchamp Racecourse, in which he finished second of the eighteen runners, beaten two lengths by Sagaro. Back in England, he won the Great Voltigeur Stakes in August, beating Irish Derby winner English Prince. At Doncaster in September, Bustino started the 11/10 favourite for the St. Leger Stakes. He was assisted by his stable companion Riboson, who set a strong pace, before Bustino took the lead in the straight and won by three lengths from Giacometti.

The Derby 1974

Snow Knight was a Thoroughbred racehorse who won Britain's most prestigious race in 1974, the Derby, then the following year earned an Eclipse Award as the American Champion Male Turf Horse. Trained by Peter Nelson, at the age of two Snow Knight made five starts, winning two and finishing second twice. At three, in the trial races for the Derby, he finished second in the Ladbrokes Classic Trial Stakes at Sandown Park and third in the Lingfield Derby Trial. Small injuries slowed him but he would fight back. Always a fractious colt, in the paddock at Epsom Downs Racecourse, Snow Knight threw jockey Brian Taylor and at the starting gate was still fighting his handlers. Sent off at odds of 50:1, he ran in the middle of the pack until the field made the turn at Tattenham Corner, when he sped to the lead and won by two lengths.

British Grand Prix 1974

The 1974 British Grand Prix (formally the John Player Grand Prix) was a Formula One motor race held at Brands Hatch on 20 July 1974. It was race 10 of 15 in both the 1974 World Championship of Drivers and the 1974 International Cup for Formula One Manufacturers. The 75-lap race was won by Jody Scheckter, driving a Tyrrell-Ford, with Emerson Fittipaldi second in a McLaren-Ford and Jacky Ickx third in a Lotus-Ford. Niki Lauda completed just 73 laps but was allowed an extra lap after the team protested his exit from the pit lane was blocked after a late wheel change. He initially classified ninth, but was awarded fifth place after appeal.

Jody David Scheckter is a South African business proprietor and former motor racing driver. He competed in Formula One from 1972 to 1980, winning the Drivers' Championship in 1979 with Ferrari. Scheckter remains the only African driver to win the Formula One World Championship and to win any World Championship Grand Prix.

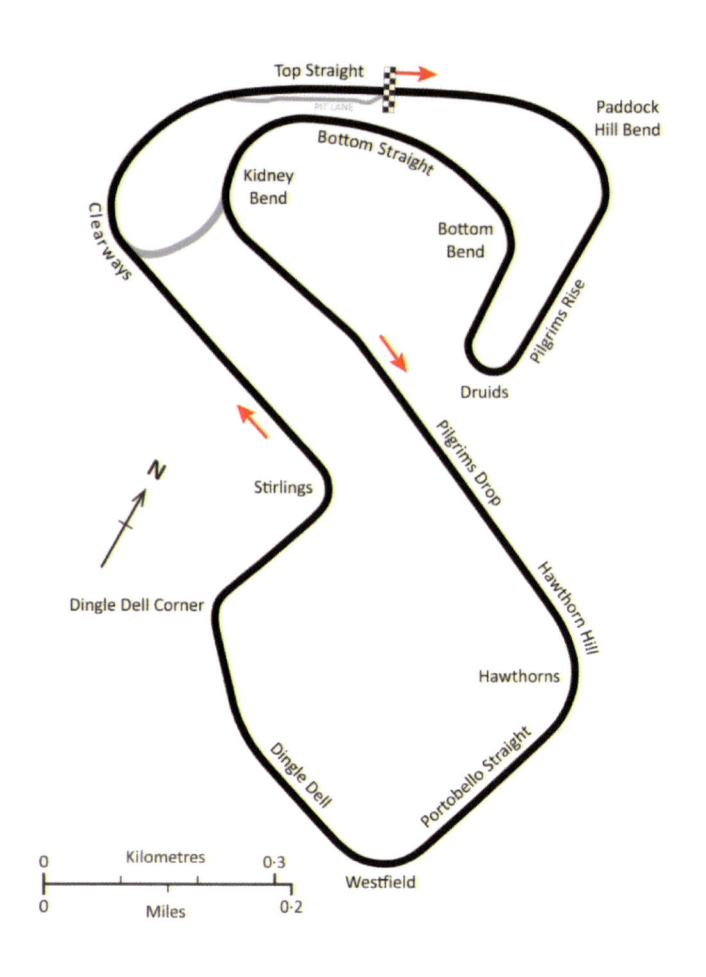

Final Placings

Pos	No	Driver	Constructor	Laps	Time/Retired	Grid	Points
1	3	Jody Scheckter	Tyrrell-Ford	75	1:43:02.2	3	9
2	5	Emerson Fittipaldi	McLaren-Ford	75	+ 15.3	8	6
3	2	Jacky Ickx	Lotus-Ford	75	+ 1:01.5	12	4
4	11	Clay Regazzoni	Ferrari	75	+ 1:07.2	7	3
5	12	Niki Lauda	Ferrari	74	+ 1 Lap	1	2
6	7	Carlos Reutemann	Brabham-Ford	74	+ 1 Lap	4	1
7	6	Denny Hulme	McLaren-Ford	74	+ 1 Lap	19	
8	16	Tom Pryce	Shadow-Ford	74	+ 1 Lap	5	
9	8	Carlos Pace	Brabham-Ford	74	+ 1 Lap	20	
10	1	Ronnie Peterson	Lotus-Ford	73	+ 2 Laps	2	

1974 Wimbledon Championships

The 1974 Wimbledon Championships was a tennis tournament that took place on the outdoor grass courts at the All England Lawn Tennis and Croquet Club in Wimbledon, London, United Kingdom. The tournament was held from Monday 24th June until Saturday 6th July 1974. It was the 88th staging of the Wimbledon Championships, and the third Grand Slam tennis event of 1974. Jimmy Connors and Chris Evert won the singles titles. The total prize money for 1974 championships was £97,100. The winner of the men's title earned £10,000 while the women's singles champion earned £7,000.

Men's Singles

Jimmy Connors defeated Ken Rosewall in the final, 6–1, 6–1, 6–4 to win the gentlemen's singles tennis title at the 1974 Wimbledon Championships. Jan Kodeš was the defending champion, but lost in the quarterfinals to Connors. Uniquely, due to the WCT ban in place at the 1972 championships and the ATP boycott of 1973, three unofficial "defending champions" competed in the event. John Newcombe, Stan Smith and Kodeš were all unbeaten from their last singles matches at the championships when this year's event commenced.

Women's Singles

Chris Evert defeated Olga Morozova in the final, 6–0, 6–4 to win the ladies' singles tennis title at the 1974 Wimbledon Championships. It was her first Wimbledon singles title and her second major singles title overall. Billie Jean King was the two-time defending champion, but lost in the quarterfinals to Morozova.

Men's Doubles

Jimmy Connors and Ilie Năstase were the defending champions, but lost in the semi-finals to John Newcombe and Tony Roche. Newcombe and Roche defeated Bob Lutz and Stan Smith in the final, 8–6, 6–4, 6–4 to win the gentlemen's doubles title at the 1974 Wimbledon Championships.

Women's Doubles

Rosie Casals and Billie Jean King were the defending champions, but lost in the quarterfinals to Helen Gourlay and Karen Krantzcke. Evonne Goolagong and Peggy Michel defeated Gourlay and Krantzcke in the final, 2–6, 6–4, 6–3 to win the ladies' doubles tennis title at the 1974 Wimbledon Championships

Mixed Doubles

Owen Davidson and Billie Jean King successfully defended their title, defeating Mark Farrell and Lesley Charles in the final, 6–3, 9–7 to win the mixed doubles tennis title at the 1974 Wimbledon Championships.

Jimmy Connors

Chris Evert

BOOKS PUBLISHED IN 1974

Aunts Aren't Gentlemen being a comic novel by P. G. Wodehouse, first published in the United Kingdom in October 1974 by Barrie & Jenkins, London, and in the United States under the title The Cat-nappers on 14 April 1975 by Simon & Schuster, New York. It was the last novel to feature some of Wodehouse's best-known characters, Bertie Wooster and his resourceful valet Jeeves, and the last novel fully completed by Wodehouse before his death. Taking place at a rural town called Maiden Eggesford, the story involves a plan by Bertie's Aunt Dahlia to kidnap a cat so that she can win a wager. The novel also chronicles the relationship between Bertie's acquaintances Orlo Porter and Vanessa Cook, and features Major Plank, whom Bertie first met in Stiff Upper Lip, Jeeves. Concerned by pink spots on his chest, Bertie goes to see E. Jimpson Murgatroyd, the Harley Street doctor recommended by his friend Tipton Plimsoll (who himself saw Murgatroyd for spots in Full Moon). On the way, Bertie sees Vanessa Cook, a headstrong girl he once proposed to but no longer wants to marry, leading a protest march. She is with her fiancé Orlo J. Porter, an acquaintance of Bertie's. Orlo and Vanessa are unable to marry since Vanessa's father, the trustee of Orlo's inheritance, refuses to give Orlo his inheritance because Orlo is a communist.

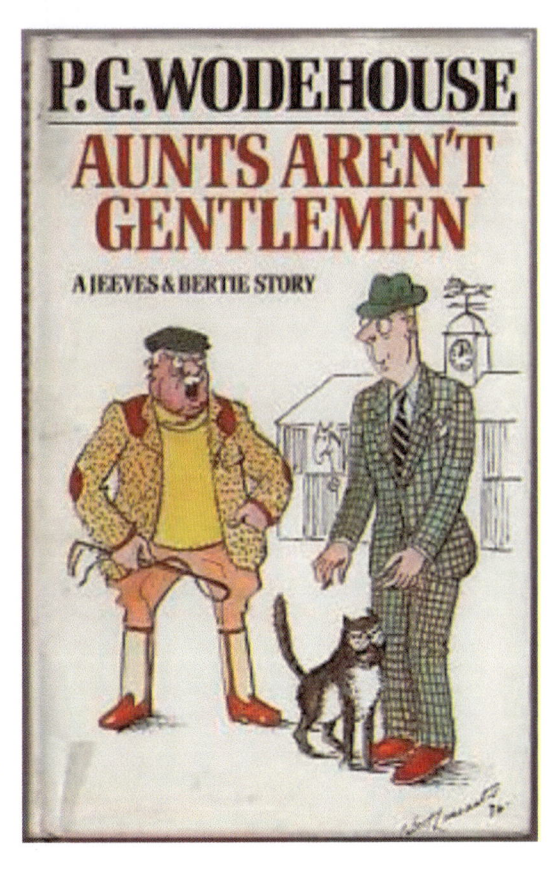

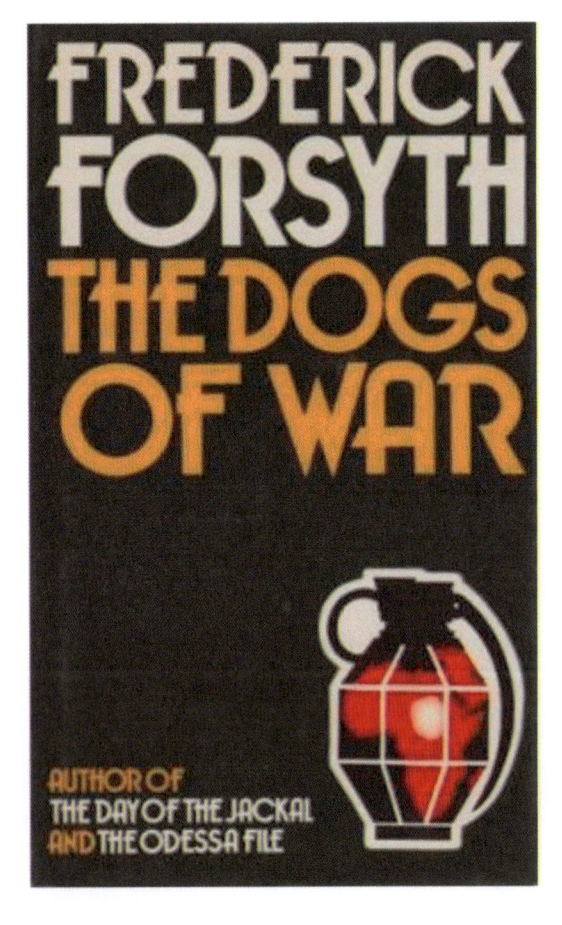

The Dogs of War (1974) is a war novel by British writer Frederick Forsyth, featuring a small group of European mercenary soldiers hired by a British industrialist to depose the government of the fictional African country of Zangaro. The story details a geologist's mineral discovery, and the preparations for the attack: soldier recruitment, training, reconnaissance, and the logistics of the coup d'état (buying weapons, transport, payment). Like most of Forsyth's work, the novel is more about the protagonists' occupational tradecraft than their characters. The source of the title, The Dogs of War, is Act III, scene 1, line 270 of Julius Caesar (1599), by William Shakespeare: Cry, 'Havoc!', and let slip the dogs of war. The mercenary protagonists are ruthless, violent anti-heroes. Initially introduced as simple killers-for-hire, they are gradually shown to adhere to a relatively moral mercenary code as the novel progresses. Forsyth draws upon his journalistic experiences in reporting the 1970 Biafran War between Biafra and Nigeria; though fictional, the African 'Republic of Zangaro' is based upon Equatorial Guinea, a former Spanish colony. The novel's dedication to five men named Giorgio, Christian, Schlee, Big Marc and Black Johnny and "the others in the unmarked graves" concludes: "at least we tried"—and alludes to Forsyth's time in Biafra; the dark tone and cynical plot of the story stem from the same source.

Flash Point is a 1974 novel by the British author Michael Gilbert published in England by Hodder and Stoughton. It was Gilbert's 17th novel and undoubtedly written during the last days of the American Watergate scandal. Although none of the events in the book directly parallel those of Watergate, it begins with a banal legal matter and then escalates into a government cover-up and national scandal.

Written with Gilbert's usual urbane and understated style, the events mostly take place in and around London, as is customary in most of his books: in sundry law offices, courts, government offices, and gentlemen's clubs. Gilbert himself was a most Establishment figure, frequently writing about other Establishment figures, and was usually firmly on the side of England's police forces and shadowy (though lethal) Intelligent departments. But perhaps because of his many years of legal practice, he was also equally at home in filling his narratives with other types of characters: sleazy strip-club owners, tough and semi-crooked policemen, hard-bitten union officials, factory workers, relentless and unscrupulous Intelligent agents, and a wide variety of hard-boiled villains and crooks from small-time burglars and con men to gangster chieftains.

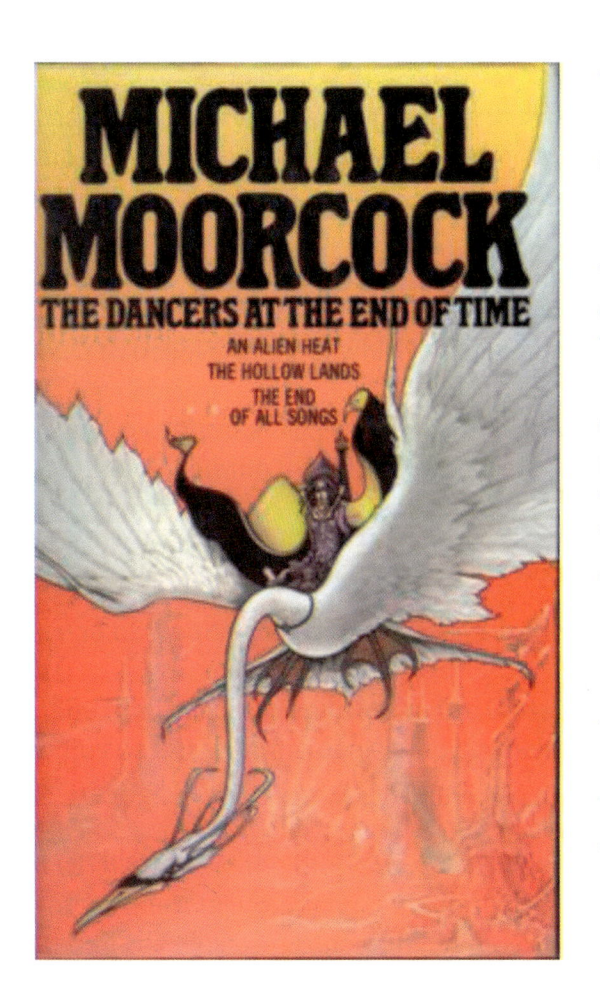

The Dancers at the End of Time is a series of science fiction novels and short stories written by Michael Moorcock, the setting of which is the End of Time, an era "where entropy is king and the universe has begun collapsing upon itself". The inhabitants of this era are immortal decadents, who create flights of fancy via the use of power rings that draw on energy devised and stored by their ancestors millions of years prior. Time travel is possible, and throughout the series various points in time are visited and revisited. Space travellers are also common, but most residents of the End of Time find leaving the planet distasteful and clichéd. The title of the series is itself taken from a poem by a fictitious 19th-century poet, Ernest Wheldrake, which Mrs. Amelia Underwood quotes in The End of All Songs. "Ernest Wheldrake" had been a pseudonym used by Algernon Charles Swinburne.

Main characters in the series include Jherek Carnelian, one of the few humans at the End of Time to have been born naturally, rather than created; Mrs Amelia Underwood, a time traveller from the late 19th century; the enigmatic Lord Jagged; and Miss Mavis Ming in the eponymous The Transformation of Miss Mavis Ming, which also features the Fireclown.

The Land Leviathan is an alternative history novel by Michael Moorcock, first published in 1974. Originally subtitled "A New Scientific Romance", it has been seen as an early steampunk novel, dealing with an alternative British Imperial history dominated by airships and futuristic warfare.

The story of Oswald Bastable's adventures "trapped forever in the shifting tides of time" is framed with the concept of the book being a long-lost manuscript, as related by Moorcock's grandfather. Several years after Bastable disappeared in 1910, the elder Moorcock travels to China in an attempt to track him down, meeting Una Persson of the Jerry Cornelius novels on the way who before disappearing leaves him a manuscript written by Bastable for Moorcock, relating what happened to Bastable after he unexpectedly left the elder Moorcock at the end of Warlord of the Air, probably bound for another alternate 20th century. Bastable's story takes in a post-apocalyptic early twentieth century between 1904 and 1908, where Western Europe and the United States have been devastated by accelerated technological change caused by a prolific Chilean inventor, which led to a prolonged global war causing their reversion to barbarism.

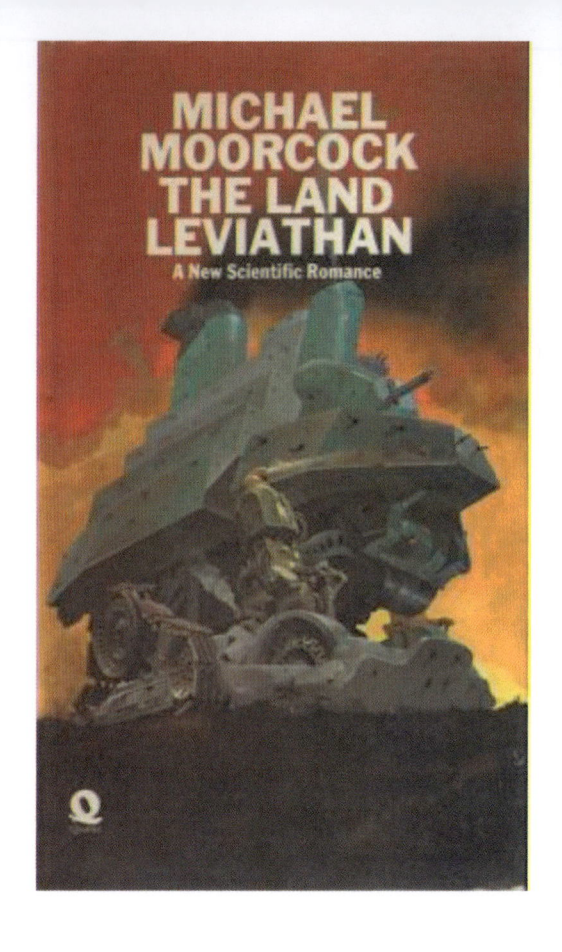

Spy Story is a 1974 spy novel by Len Deighton, which features minor characters from his earlier novels The IPCRESS File, Funeral in Berlin, Horse Under Water, and Billion Dollar Brain.

The story opens with Armstrong and his colleague Ferdy Foxwell returning from a six-week mission aboard a nuclear submarine, gathering data on Soviet communications and electronic warfare techniques in the Arctic Ocean. He and Foxwell visit "The Bonnet", a rural Scottish public house. On returning to London, Armstrong's car breaks down on his way home and he decides to use the phone in his old flat, for which he still has the key. He is surprised and disturbed to discover that the flat has been refurnished, including photographs which he owns but with someone else replacing him in the images, wearing identical clothes. He discovers a door hidden in the back of the wardrobe leading into the adjoining flat, which has been fitted out as some kind of sick bay. When he leaves the flat thinking that a taxi he ordered has arrived, he is confronted by Special Branch officers who have a former member of the Studies Centre verify who he is before releasing him.

MOVIES 1974

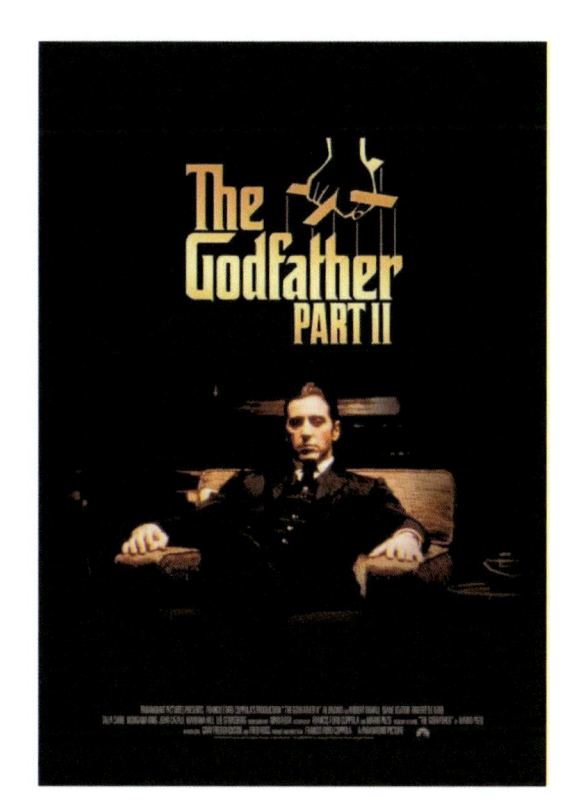

The Godfather Part II. The continuation of the Godfather saga with two focuses: the ongoing story of the Corleone family, and Michael in particular, and Vito Corleone's (Michael's father) backstory. Regarding the ongoing Michael Corleone story, it is about seven years since the events that concluded The Godfather. With the murders of the heads of the other four New York / New Jersey families, the Corleone family has unassailable control in New York. The move to Nevada went smoothly and Michael Corleone controls several hotels and casinos in the state. Frank Pentageli, the man who runs Michael's interests in New York, comes to Michael, asking if he can take out the Rosato Brothers as they are infringing on Pentageli's turf and business interests. However, the Rosatos are backed by Hyman Roth, a business partner of Michael's and a long-time ally of Michael's father, Vito Corleone, and Michael refuses. An attempted assassination attempt is then carried out on Michael's life, in his own home.

Run time is 3h 22mins

Trivia

Robert De Niro spent four months learning to speak the Sicilian dialect of Italian in order to play Vito Corleone. Nearly all of the dialogue that his character speaks in the film was in Sicilian.

Originally, the actors in the flashback scenes wore pants with zippers. One of the musicians pointed out that the zipper had not been invented at that time, so some scenes had to be re-shot with button-fly trousers.

Francis Ford Coppola had a horrible time directing The Godfather (1972) and asked to pick a different director for the sequel, while taking the title of producer for himself. He chose Martin Scorsese, who the film executives rejected. Thus, Coppola agreed to direct the film, with a few conditions.

Goofs

During Roth's birthday party, the pattern on his shirt changes. Due to weather difficulties, the two-minute scene took over a week to shoot and the original shirt was lost at some point. The production designer attempted to recreate it by drawing an approximation of the pattern onto a plain shirt, but it didn't quite match.

Shortly after the assassination attempt on Michael in his bedroom, he meets alone in a room with Tom Hagen. They sit at an empty table. After talking for a few minutes, Michael offers Tom a glass of Courvoisier, from a bottle which has randomly materialized on the table.

When Vito Corleone arrives at Ellis Island, he was marked with a circled X (historically X was a sign for a mental illness), not because he was suspected to have smallpox, but because he was a nine-year-old who did not speak. Even deaf people at the time were frequently labelled as "retarded" simply because they did not speak.

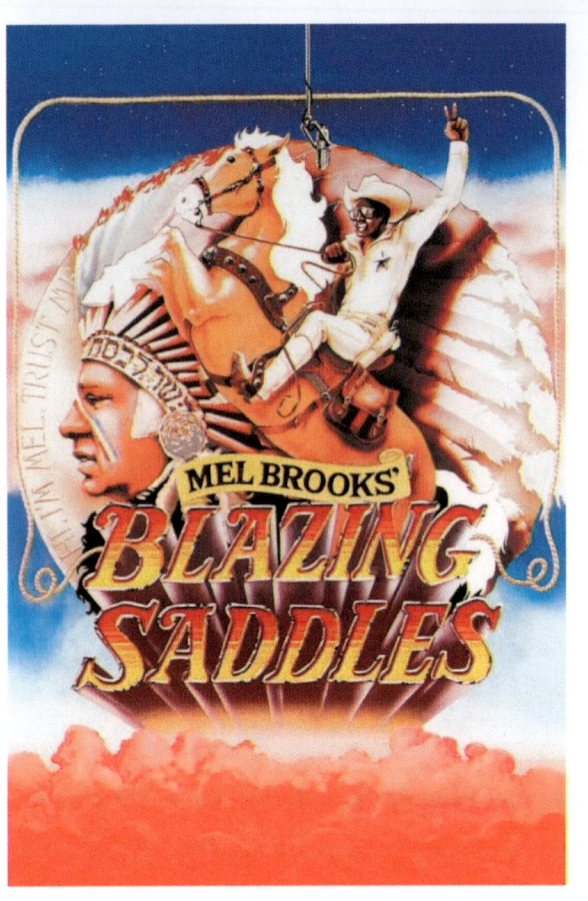

Blazing Saddles. It's 1874 in the American frontier of the wild west. Because of geological problems, a railroad under construction needs to be rerouted through the town of Rock Ridge, where general lawlessness prevails, that lawlessness which led to the town sheriff being murdered. Upon learning this information from Taggart - the railroad construction boss and secretly his right-hand man - Hedley Lamarr, the state attorney and assistant to hapless Governor William J. Le Petomane, senses an opportunity to make millions by acquiring as much property in Rock Ridge as possible before the news of the railroad gets to residents of the town which would encourage them to stay despite the lawlessness. Hedley's ultimate plan, which he has to devise upon learning that the residents have decided to stay and which he is able to enact, is to get the Governor to appoint a new sheriff - the town elders having asked him to do so - so offensive to the townsfolk that they will voluntarily leave town without any prompting. Hedley's choice of that new sheriff is a man named Bart, who was part of the railroad construction gang, and who Hedley was going to hang on Taggart's initiative solely because of an antagonistic encounter between the two.

Run time 1h 33m

Trivia

Before shooting, Gene Hackman and Al Pacino both dressed as hobos and hitchhiked through California to get into their characters.

According to Al Pacino, he and Gene Hackman did not get along very well during filming due to their different personalities.

According to Jerry Schatzberg, Gene Hackman was hard to work with and argued with everyone on the set including his brother, Richard Hackman, who was working as his stand-in. To get back at Gene, Schatzberg gave Richard a part in the film, but Gene ended up being delighted that his brother was in the film.

Gene Hackman was asked in a rare interview about his favourite movie of all the ones he did. He said it's really hard to pick; it's just like picking one of your children. However, he said, " ...there was a movie I did years ago; didn't get much press; it was called Scarecrow."

The film was entered and selected to screen in competition at the Cannes Film Festival in 1973 where the picture won in a tie the prestigious Palme d'Or (The Golden Palm) award shared with Alan Bridges' The Hireling (1973).

The actor sharing a table with Richard Lynch (Riley) at the work farm commissary is Tony Lo Bianco. The two of them were in The Seven-Ups (1973) the same year this film was released, and they worked together again a couple years later in God Told Me To (1976)" as extra-terrestrial siblings. Lo Bianco also appeared in The French Connection (1971) with Gene Hackman.

On the set, Gene Hackman and Al Pacino had different ways of preparing for a scene. The former actor would remain focused and silent, whereas the latter would become tense and energetic.

Chinatown. In 1937 Los Angeles, private investigator Jake 'J.J.' Gittes specializes in cheating-spouse cases. His current target is Hollis Mulwray, high-profile chief engineer for the Los Angeles Department of Water and Power, whose wife suspects him of infidelity. In following Mulwray, Gittes witnesses some usual business dealings, such as a public meeting for construction of a new dam to create additional water supply for Los Angeles, as fresh water is vital to the growing community during the chronic drought; Mulwray opposes the dam. Eventually Gittes sees Mulwray meeting with an unknown young woman who isn't his wife. Once news of the supposed tryst between Mulwray and this woman hits the media, additional information comes to light that makes Gittes believe that Mulwray is being framed for something and that he himself is being set up. In his investigation of the issue behind Mulwray's framing and his own setup, Gittes is assisted by Mulwray's wife Evelyn, but he thinks she isn't being forthright with him. The further he gets into the investigation, the more secrets he uncovers about the Mulwrays' professional and personal dealings.

Runtime 2h 10mins

Trivia

At the time of filming, Jack Nicholson had just embarked on his longstanding relationship with Anjelica Huston. This made his scenes with her father, John Huston, rather uncomfortable, especially as the only time Anjelica was on set was the day they were filming the scene where Noah Cross interrogates Nicholson's character with "Mr. Gittes...do you sleep with my daughter?"

After several takes that never looked quite right, Faye Dunaway got annoyed and told Jack Nicholson to actually slap her. He did and felt very guilty for it, despite it being Dunaway's decision. The shot made it into the movie.

Screenwriter Robert Towne was originally offered $125,000 to write a screenplay for The Great Gatsby (1974), but Towne felt he couldn't do better than F. Scott Fitzgerald novel and accepted $25,000 to write his own story, "Chinatown," instead.

Goofs

Gittes lights a cigarette while waiting to see Yelburton for the second time. Entering his office, he takes a puff, but when they shake hands, the cigarette is gone.

In the orange grove scene, Gittes's car has its right front tire shot and deflated, yet it is not deflated when the car hits the tree.

When Gittes gets in a fight with the owners of the farmland, one of the lenses of Gittes's sunglasses comes off. However, in the last shot Gittes is laying down with the sunglasses intact.

When Cross and Gittes are lunching, the close-up of Jake's plate does not match, with the fish, potatoes, and lemon wedge being in completely different positions.

The Texas Chain Saw Massacre. The year is 1974. A group of five close friends are heading through the back roads of Texas en route to their grandfather's potentially vandalized grave. Among them are Sally Hardesty, and her invalid brother Franklin. They encounter an unpleasant hitchhiker (Neal) who slashes both himself & Franklin with a wicked-looking knife. The others manage to eject the hitchhiker from the vehicle, but shortly after wards, they are forced to stop & wander over to a small, sinister clapboard house nearby in hopes for gas. What none of them realize is that this house is the home of the ghoulish Leatherface (Hansen) and his evil, demented family of cannibalistic psychopaths. One at a time, the teens are murdered by the Leatherface in horrifying ways. Sally soon finds herself an involuntary guest at Leatherface's home, and flees into the night to escape the demented cannibal and his loudly-buzzing chainsaw. Can she escape the grim fate that befell her friends & brother? Based on the terrifying true story of Ed Gein.

Runtime 1h 23mins

Trivia
Marilyn Burns, whose character was chased by Leatherface through the undergrowth, actually cut herself on the branches quite badly, so a lot of the blood on her body and clothes is real.

The soundtrack contains no sounds from musical instruments (with the exception of some copyrighted music they had the rights to), instead they used sounds an animal would hear inside a slaughterhouse.

Even in his lift boots, Gunnar Hansen could run faster than Marilyn Burns, so he had to do random things when chasing her through the woods (you'll notice in one head-on shot that he starts slicing up tree branches in the background).

Tobe Hooper used a stunt double for Sally's leap through the window, but, Marilyn Burns actually hurt herself shooting the insert of her falling to the ground.

Goofs
When Leatherface chases Sally into the house the first time and she escapes through an upstairs window, he corners her on the stairs and she leaps out a window off the hallway on the second floor. However, when Leatherface appears in the empty window frame after she jumps, he's standing in an attic window with a gable.

When the Hitchhiker has been thrown out of the van and proceeds to chase after, and smear blood on the side of the van, at one point the camera cuts to the inside of the van to show the hitchhiker blowing raspberries through the window at the teenagers. During these perspectives, a clapper board, and a crew member wearing a red t-shirt, can be seen reflected in the window.

After the hitch hiker cuts his own hand, he laughs and waves the knife. Watch carefully and you can see the hose behind the blade the blood came through.

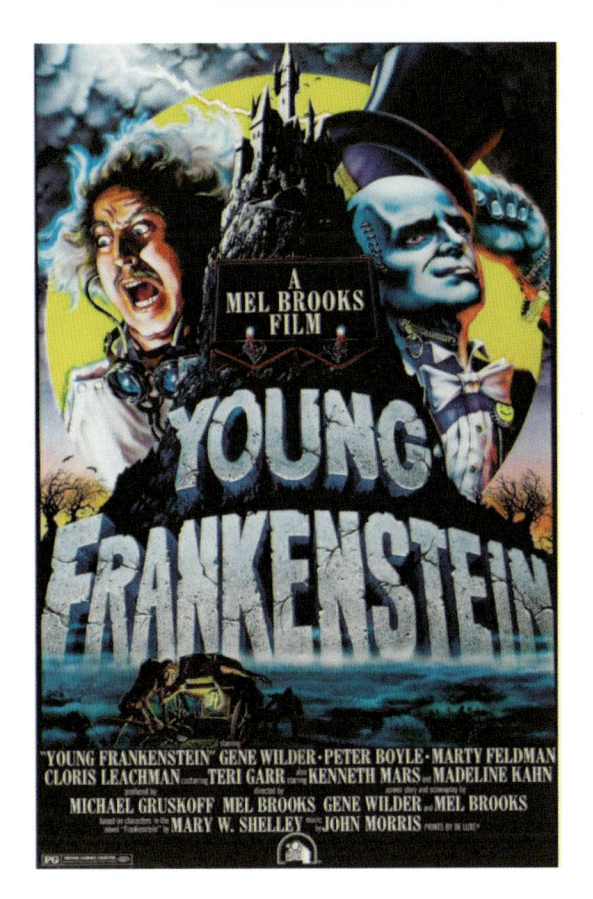

Young Frankenstein. As a respected researcher and physician, Dr. Frederick Frankenstein, the grandson of the more famous Dr. Victor Frankenstein, who did experiments on bringing back the dead, tries to disassociate himself from his more famous relative, even to the point of pronouncing their surname differently. Regardless, Frederick is drawn back to the small Transylvannian town and castle where Victor conducted his experiments, he leaving behind his somewhat standoffish and "untouchable" fiancée, Elizabeth, back in the US. He also slowly begins to get drawn into the research that his grandfather conducted, he eventually learns not by accident. As Frederick tries to reanimate his dead subject with the help of his hunchbacked aide Igor and his beautiful assistant Inga, rumours abound in the town of what he is doing, they who have been trying to disassociate themselves from the work of the former Dr. Frankenstein generations ago. Inspector Kemp is tasked with stopping any work if it is indeed happening. All these issues collide as Frederick and team try to hide their work from the Inspector while hitting some technical roadblocks, and as Elizabeth comes to Transylvania and accidentally gets caught up in the experiment.

Runtime 1h 46mins

Trivia

When Mel Brooks was preparing for this film, he discovered that Ken Strickfaden, who'd made the elaborate electrical machinery for the lab sequences in the Universal Frankenstein films, was still alive and living in the Los Angeles area. Brooks visited Strickfaden, and found that he had stored all the equipment in his garage. Brooks made a deal to rent the equipment, and gave Strickfaden the screen credit he didn't receive for the original films.

The shifting hump on Igor's back was an ad-libbed gag. Marty Feldman had been surreptitiously shifting the hump back and forth for several days when cast members finally noticed. It was then added to the script.

Gene Hackman ad-libbed The Blind Man's parting line "I was gonna make espresso." The scene immediately fades to black because the crew erupted into fits of laughter. Hackman was unable to repeat the line without laughing with the rest of the crew, so the first take was used. Hackman was uncredited when the movie was originally released in theatres.

Goofs

When the criminal is being hanged, it's raining heavily. When he's buried, the gravediggers are shovelling dry, almost dusty soil onto the grave. When Frederick and Igor dig him up, the mud on their clothes and the coffin is soaking wet and water can be seen dripping down near where Frederick had been lifting. This may have been intentional for Igor's "could be raining" line.

The candle that operates the bookcase door appears to go out momentarily, and then comes back on, before Frankenstein and the assistant go down the passageway, but it simply got caught in a draft and dimmed completely down before coming up again - normal behaviour of candles.

In the dart throwing scene, the first dart lands in a "7" space and the rest near the bull's-eye. After a cut-away, the dart in the "7" spot is missing.

The Man with the Golden Gun. Francisco Scaramanga, a hitman who is known as "the man with the golden gun", because of the golden gun he carries, and the gold bullets he uses on his targets. Bond receives a message supposedly from Scaramanga saying that Bond is his next target.

M decides to relieve Bond of his duties until the danger has been neutralized. But Bond, feeling that the mission he was on is of the utmost urgency, decides to go and find Scaramanga, and he thinks he found him, but discovers that Scaramanga is not after him when he had a clear shot at him and missed, which he doesn't do. But the man who was killed is the man for whom he was originally looking.

A scientist working on a device that can make harnessing the sun's energy possible. So, he must now find the device.

Run time 2h 05mins

Trivia

In his autobiography, Sir Roger Moore said that when they were filming the boat chase on the klongs, he fell in twice. The first was on purpose (because they told him not to do it), and the second time was by accident. On the second fall, Moore made the mistake of opening his eyes underwater, and saw what the local undertakers did with the bodies of the less fortunate. Conversely, this is the only Sir Roger Moore Bond movie where the Bond character is not drenched in water in some way.

One of the lowest grossing Bond movies. That fact, combined with behind-the-scenes problems, nearly made this the final Bond movie, and delayed production of the next entry in the franchise, The Spy Who Loved Me (1977).

The title role was originally offered to Jack Palance, before it eventually went to Sir Christopher Lee, the cousin of Ian Fleming who was known as the Man with the Golden Pen (Fleming had previously wanted Lee in the title role in Dr. No (1962)).

Goofs

After Goodnight is locked in the boot of the car she tells Bond where she is, Bond and Hip go to their car as Scaramanga drives past them, they then discover that they have not got the car keys and Goodnight tells them (on the radio) that she has it a passage of time lasting many seconds, Bond and Hip then get out of the car to see that the car which Goodnight is in has only moved a couple of feet.

When Nick Nack is at his console watching Scaramanga in his 'Funhouse' he has screens showing different sections of it. When we see the cameras, they are all panning constantly from side to side. However, all the shots on Nick Nack's screens are static shots of one angle.

During the car chase scene between Bond and Scaramanga, the villain's car first has a noticeable dent in the lower part of the passenger-side door. Seconds later, the dent has disappeared.

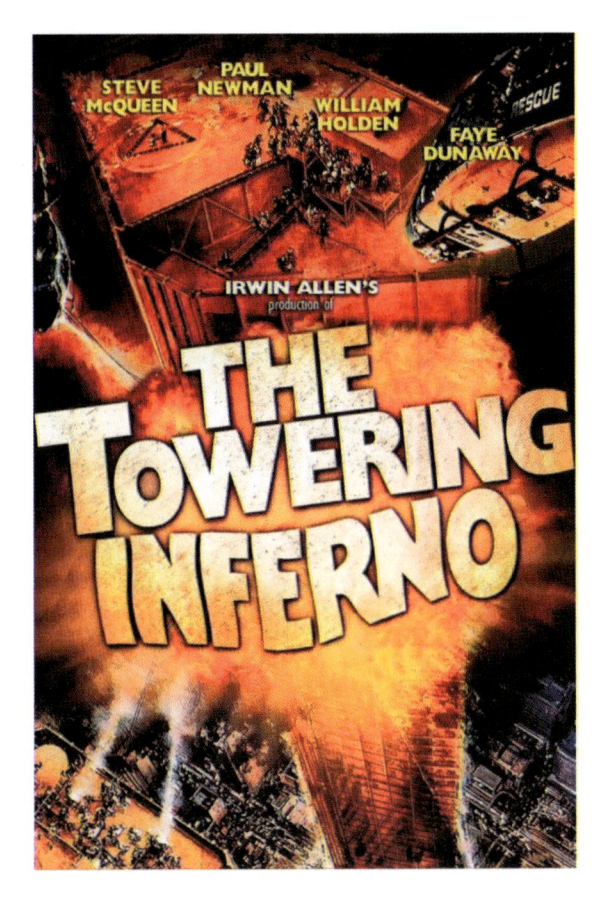

The Towering Inferno. "The Towering Inferno," one in a string of disaster movies of the 1970s, was promoted as a tribute to firefighters and their heroic work. It was also among the highest-grossing box office draws of the mid-1970s. The finishing touches have just been made to the Glass Tower, a 138-story skyscraper in the heart of San Francisco. A huge celebratory gala, complete with VIP guests, has been planned to celebrate the dedication of what has been promoted as the world's tallest building. But the building's architect, Doug Roberts, suspects all is not right with the building. The contractors have used shoddy wiring, not the heavy-duty wiring he had specified. The overworked wiring develops short circuits, coincidentally enough during the height of the celebratory extravaganza; it isn't long before the Glass Tower becomes a huge towering inferno. The nearly 300 guests become trapped on the building's 135th floor, where the party takes place. Fire Chief Michael O'Halloran immediately devises a daring plan to rescue the trapped guests, but his efforts quickly become a battle against time and the panicked guests.

Run time 1h 45m

Trivia

Both novels were inspired by the construction of the World Trade Centre in the early-1970s, and what could happen in a fire in a skyscraper. In Richard Martin Stern's novel "The Tower", the fictional 125-story building was set next to the north tower of the World Trade Centre. The climax of the novel was centred around a rescue mounted from the north tower.

During filming an actual fire broke out on one of the sets and Steve McQueen found himself briefly helping real firefighters put it out. One of the firefighters, not recognizing McQueen, said to the actor, "My wife is not going to believe this", to which McQueen replied, "Neither is mine."

Desperate to capture a truly surprised reaction from the cast, Irwin Allen actually fired a handgun into the ceiling without warning the actors, who were understandably "surprised". The trick worked and he got his shot.

Goofs

At the end of the movie the tower seems to be well lit despite the power outage caused by the fire.

When the fire trucks are en route to the Glass Tower, they pass the same AMC dealership three times. Twice they pass it with the dealership on their left, once with it on their right, which couldn't happen unless the trucks were driving in circles.

When OHallaran and the firefighters are in the elevator shaft getting ready to repel down to 65, a firefighter on fire falls past them in the shaft, when the firefighter first passes them it looks like they're attached to the elevator cables, and in the next shot, that same firefighter is now in freefall with no cables visible.

Death Wish. A New York City architect becomes a one-man vigilante squad after his wife is murdered by street punks. In self-defence, the vengeful man kills muggers on the mean streets after dark. Living a peaceful and happy life with his supportive wife and their grown-up daughter, Paul Kersey, a successful architect and once a conscientious objector, seems to have everything. Then a brutal home invasion by a sadistic gang of street thugs in his Manhattan apartment robs pacifist Paul of everything he holds dear, leaving a bitter taste in his mouth when he realizes that the efforts of the local police department to find the culprits are fruitless. As the sense of injustice gives way to an irrepressible desire for retribution, the once quiet family man summons up the courage to take the law into his own hands and become an executioner bent on cleaning New York's mean streets with his deadly .32 caliber Colt Police Positive revolver. And now that Kersey has tasted the forbidden fruit of vigilante justice, no mugger or killer can hide away from him. Will Paul Kersey, the man with the death wish, ever stop his bloody one-man crusade?

Runtime 1h 33 mins

Trivia

After finishing The Stone Killer (1973), Charles Bronson and Michael Winner wanted to make another film together, and were discussing further projects. "What do we do next?" asked Bronson. "The best script I've got is 'Death Wish'. It's about a man whose wife and daughter are mugged and he goes out and shoots muggers," said Winner. "I'd like to do that," Bronson said. "The film?" asked Winner. Bronson replied, "No . . . shoot muggers."

The name "Paul Kersey" was the actual name of one of the extras hired for the movie. He allowed the use of his name in exchange for his appearing in all possible scenes requiring an extra.

The role of Paul Kersey was originally intended for Steve McQueen, who turned it down.

Goofs

During the funeral, there is a shot of Paul with his daughter and son-and-law. The next shot is of Sam and Ives with their spouses holding an umbrella. Next to the four of them is an extra in a brown coat, blue pants, and white shirt. The next shot shows the priest reading from a Bible, and here, the same extra is seen in the background on the opposite side of the group.

When Paul Kersey is about to be robbed in the subway wagon, a big brown shopping bag can be seen. In the next scene, when he leaves the wagon, the bag is gone. It is the same shopping bag that is later referred to in the police station.

The inspector's assistant is told to wait in front of Kersey's apartment building at 33 Riverside Drive. When the inspector returns he is in front of a door marked 322.

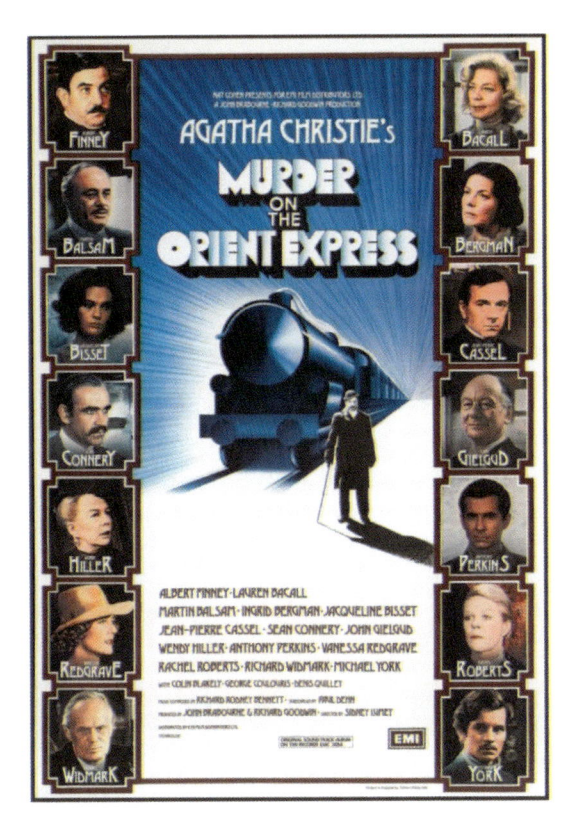

Murder on the Orient Express. The first-class compartment of the December 1935 departure of the Orient Express from Istanbul is full, unusual for this time of the year. Regardless, famed and fastidious Belgian detective, Hercule Poirot, who needs to get back to London immediately, is able to secure last minute passage in the compartment with the assistance of his friend, Signor Bianchi, one of the directors of the train line who is also making the trip. Some of the first-class passengers seem concerned about Poirot's presence on the train. At least one of them has reason to be concerned, as later, another first-class passenger, who earlier in the trip asked Poirot to provide protection for him due to several death threats, is found murdered in his stateroom by multiple stabbings. At the time the victim is found, the train is unexpectedly stopped and delayed due to snow in remote Yugoslavia, which may be problematic for the murderer in getting away now that Poirot is on the case, which he is doing as a favour to Bianchi as not to get the Yugoslav police involved.

Run time 2h 08m

Trivia

84-year-old Agatha Christie attended the movie premiere in November 1974. It was the only movie adaptation in her lifetime with which she was completely satisfied. In particular, she felt that Albert Finney's performance came closest to her idea of Poirot (though she was reportedly unimpressed with his too-subtle moustache). The premiere was her final public appearance. She died fourteen months later, on January 12, 1976.

In 1929, a westbound Orient Express train was stuck in snow for five days at Çerkezköy, approximately one hundred thirty kilometres (eighty-one miles) from Istanbul, Turkey. This incident inspired the setting of the book and movie.

The luxury food that is inspected and carried aboard the train had been stolen from the set just before shooting. All of the food had to be bought again, in the middle of the night, on-location in Paris, France.

Goofs

As Poirot goes to leave the car after announcing his solution to the murder, Pierre is shown opening the salon door, and holding it open as Poirot pauses in the doorway, turns and watches as the various passengers make toasts to one another. Pierre is the first to step up and raise a toast with his glass of champagne. But when all the toasts have been made, Poirot is shown still standing in the doorway, then turning to exit, even as Pierre (actually just his arm is visible, but it couldn't have been anyone else) is seen in the exact same position, still holding open the door for Poirot.

When Poirot uses the hat box to decode the burnt paper, in one shot Poirot places his small burning lamp to his right. In the next shot, the lamp is in the centre ready for the hat frames to be placed over it.

In the end credits, Wendy Hiller is credited as Wendy Miller.

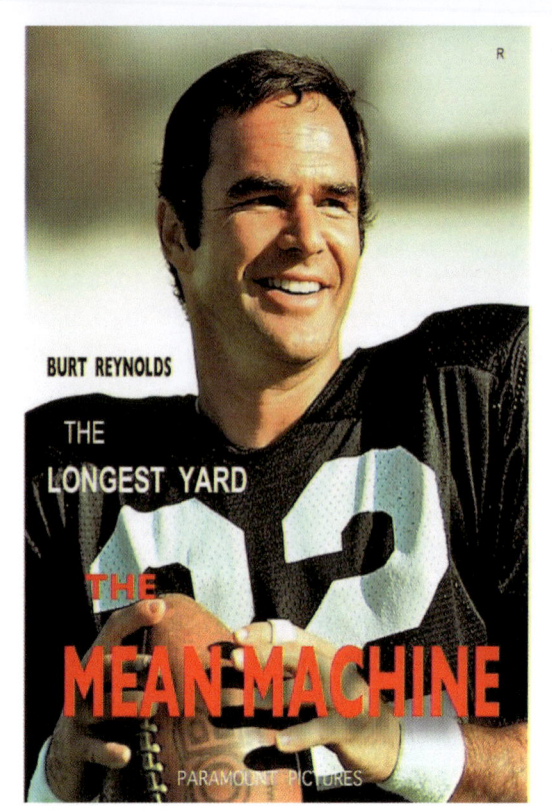

The Mean Machine. An ex-football player Paul Crewe (Reynolds) spirals out after being caught shaving points to gamble on games. Some bad choices lead to Crewe getting sent to prison where the warden has his eye on him to coach their semi pro team. After refusing, at the lead guards forceful request, Crewe finds himself in the dregs of the prison workforce. Finally, the warden decides to use him in a different capacity and tasks him with putting together an all inmate football team to play a tune up game with the guards. Through trials and tribulations, Crewe gets his team together and puts the guards through their paces in an all-out roughed out guard on inmate football game.

Box office
Budget
$2,900,000 (estimated)

Gross worldwide
$43,008,075

Run time 2h 01m

Trivia

Producer Albert S. Ruddy says that his inspiration for the film came from a friend of his who was a promising football player. After a career-ending injury, his life took a downward spiral. He was working a minimum-wage job at a sandwich shop and was being mistreated by his snobbish girlfriend. Ruddy took the scenario from there.

Burt Reynolds' brother is the player wearing black jersey #65 seen running beside Reynolds in the final play of the game.

Actor Richard Keil is too big for the Mean Machine helmet in the dressing room scene where you can see him struggling to fit a normal helmet and failing. Later in the game scenes you can clearly see his helmet is a different design to the other players.

Goofs

After Paul backs the car off of the rising drawbridge, the rear end is smashed, and the trunk lid is flapping up and down. When he drives it down to the bay to dunk it in the water, the trunk lid is securely closed.

After the first time that Crewe hits Bogdanski "below the belt" with the football, the game clock has stopped at 2:29 remaining in the game, after the second time he does it, the clock is at 2:35 remaining and running.

After Scarboro scores his touchdown, he is taken out by a guard who hits him in his left knee. But when he is brought into the infirmary, his right knee is bandaged.

While they are playing the football game, towards the beginning and again as the game is won, they show inmates celebrating in their cells, but reuse the video from the earlier scenes when Unger had booby trapped Crewe's jail cell light bulb to explode. The smoke from the earlier fire can be seen filling the far end of the shot in all the scenes.

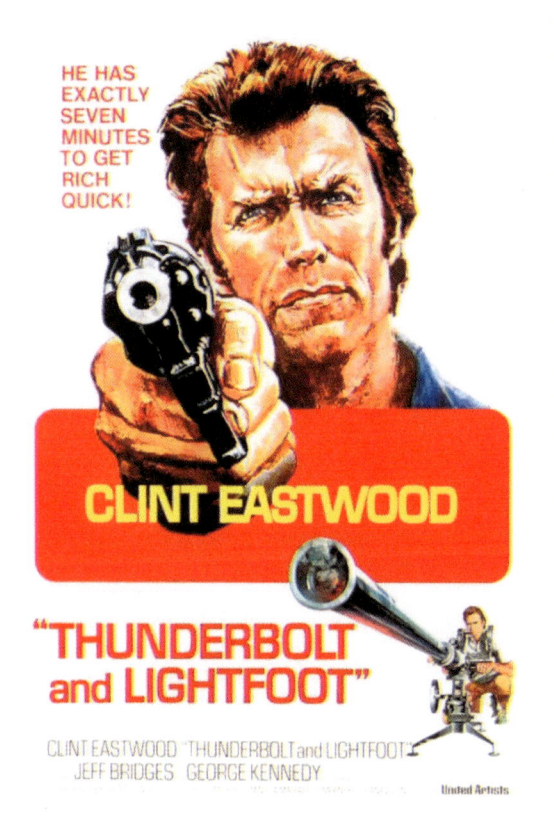

Thunderbolt and Lightfoot. A middle-aged man nicknamed Thunderbolt (Clint Eastwood) has been masquerading as a preacher at a church located in the western American countryside. When he is found by one of the many who know who he really is, Thunderbolt is able to escape when he literally runs into a twenty-something man nicknamed Lightfoot (Jeff Bridges) (in reality, when Lightfoot runs into him). Despite not knowing anything about the other, the two decide to hang out together since they seem to have a similar temperament as two good old boys who have a penchant for doing things to bring them on the wrong side of the law. As they travel the American west together, there are people on their tail trying to kill them. When Lightfoot brings up the topic of robbing a bank, Thunderbolt's true history comes to light: he's a bank robber whose last job netted five hundred thousand dollars still hidden where only he of the surviving team members knows. The media reported that the money had been recovered, which, in reality, was a sting operation by the Police to draw out the robbers.

Run Time 2hr 31mins

Trivia

When writer and director Michael Cimino was discussing this movie with Jeff Bridges, he told Bridges it was his job to make Clint Eastwood laugh both on and off-camera, and he did.

According to Steven Bach's "Final Cut", Clint Eastwood was disappointed with this movie's initial disappointing $9 million receipts, and blamed United Artists for inadequately promoting the movie. Despite his relationship with the studio on the Spaghetti Westerns, and a two-movie deal from the studio, he never made another movie for them.

The small boy in blue shirt and cap at the ice-cream truck (at ~44 min.) is Clint Eastwood's son Kyle Eastwood, 5 years old at the time. Like the other extras he earned $25 for the appearance, not including the ice cream cone Clint hands him in the scene.

Goofs

After the crazy guy rolls the black Plymouth, you can see damage to the drivers side roof and the rear wheel on the driver side is bent at extreme angle and the passenger side rear wheel completely flies off the axle. However, moments later when Thunderbolt and Lightfoot are going down the road neither signs of damage are apparent.

During the chase where Thunderbolt and Lightfoot are driving the Buick Riviera. you see the other guys put a silencer on his gun, but you hear gunfire that should be muffled but isn't.

After Thunderbolt has sex with Gloria and she demands that he drive her home, the shots of Eastwood with the "bullet wound" on his right chest is revealed to be what it is, a plastic make-up application that is also peeling off.

There was a lot of money behind the blackboard but Lightfoot only had a small satchel of money with him at the end.

MUSIC 1974

Artist	Single	Week ending date	Weeks at number one
The New Seekers	"You Won't Find Another Fool Like Me"	19 January 1974	1
Mud	"Tiger Feet"	26 January 1974	4
Suzi Quatro	"Devil Gate Drive"	23 February 1974	2
Alvin Stardust	"Jealous Mind"	9 March 1974	1
Paper Lace	"Billy Don't Be a Hero"	16 March 1974	3
Terry Jacks	"Seasons in the Sun"	6 April 1974	4
ABBA	"Waterloo"	4 May 1974	2
The Rubettes	"Sugar Baby Love"	18 May 1974	4
Ray Stevens	"The Streak"	15 June 1974	1
Gary Glitter	"Always Yours"	22 June 1974	1
Charles Aznavour	"She"	29 June 1974	4
George McCrae	"Rock Your Baby"	27 July 1974	3
The Three Degrees	"When Will I See You Again"	17 August 1974	2
The Osmonds	"Love Me for a Reason"	31 August 1974	3
Carl Douglas	"Kung Fu Fighting"	21 September 1974	3
John Denver	"Annie's Song"	12 October 1974	1
Sweet Sensation	"Sad Sweet Dreamer"	19 October 1974	1
Ken Boothe	"Everything I Own"	26 October 1974	3
David Essex	"Gonna Make You a Star"	16 November 1974	3
Barry White	"You're the First, the Last, My Everything"	7 December 1974	2
Mud	"Lonely This Christmas"	21 December 1974	4

The UK Singles Chart is the official record chart in the United Kingdom. In the 1970s, it was compiled weekly by the British Market Research Bureau (BMRB) on behalf of the British record industry with a one-week break each Christmas. Prior to 1969 many music papers compiled their own sales charts but, on 15th February 1969, the BMRB was commissioned in a joint venture by the BBC and Record Retailer to compile the chart. BMRB compiled the first chart from postal returns of sales logs from 250 record shops. The sampling cost approximately £52,000 and shops were randomly chosen and submitted figures for sales taken up to the close of trade on Saturday. The data was compiled on Monday and given to the BBC on Tuesday to be announced on Johnnie Walker's afternoon show and later published in Record Retailer (rebranded Music Week in 1972). However, the BMRB often struggled to have the full sample of sales figures returned by post. The 1971 postal strike meant that data had to be collected by telephone but this was deemed inadequate for a national chart, and by 1973 the BMRB was using motorcycle couriers to collect sales figures.

New Seekers

"You Won't Find Another Fool Like Me"

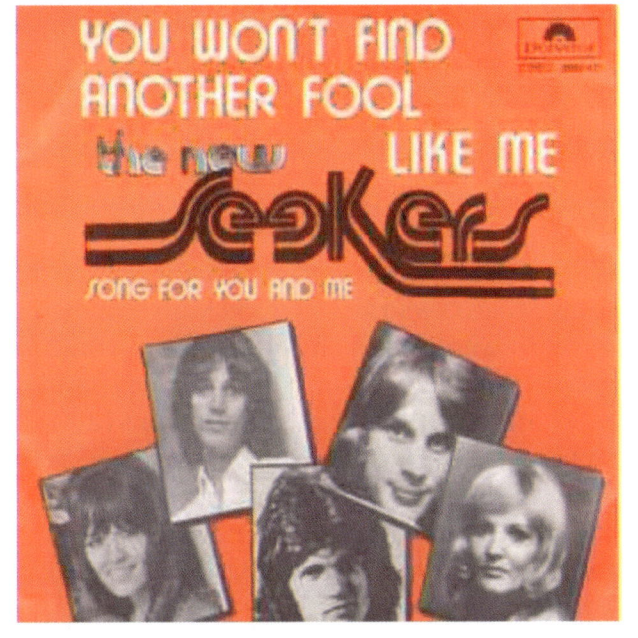

"You Won't Find Another Fool Like Me" is a 1973 single by British pop group The New Seekers. Written by Tony Macaulay and Geoff Stephens, arranged by Gerry Shury and produced by Tommy Oliver.

Featuring lead vocals by member Lyn Paul (the first time she had sung lead on a single), the song became the group's biggest hit for two years as it remained in the top five over Christmas 1973. "You Won't Find Another Fool Like Me" went on to be the band's second and final number-one single in the UK Singles Chart, spending a single week at the top of the chart in January 1974.

The song was included on the group's final album as an active band, Together, as they announced their decision to split a month later.

Mud

"Tiger Feet"

"Tiger Feet" is a popular song by the English glam rock band Mud, released in January 1974. Written and produced by the song writing team of Mike Chapman and Nicky Chinn, it was the first of three number No. 1 singles for the band, in the UK Singles Chart. followed later that year by "Lonely This Christmas", and then in 1975 by "Oh Boy!". The band appeared on Top of the Pops wearing tiger slippers.

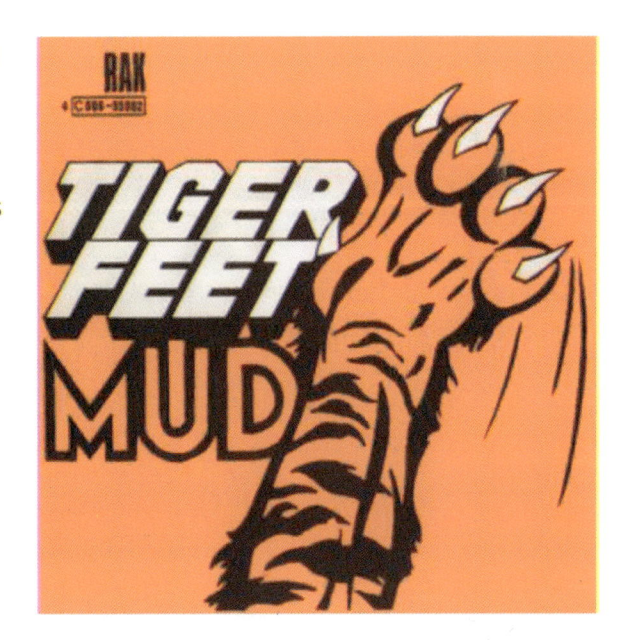

Co-writer and producer Mike Chapman credited bassist Ray Stiles with a particularly memorable bass lick which helped fuel the success of the record.

It sold over 700,000 copies in the UK alone and over a million copies globally. It was also the best-selling single in Britain that year.

Suzi Quatro

"Devil Gate Drive"

"**Devil Gate Drive**" is a song by American singer Suzi Quatro. It was Quatro's second (and final) solo number one single in the UK, spending two weeks at the top of the chart in February 1974. According to ukcharts.20m.com, she only reached number one again, in the UK, 13 years and 26 days later (as part of the Ferry Aid band in a charity version of the Lennon–McCartney song "Let It Be").

Written and produced by Nicky Chinn and Mike Chapman, "Devil Gate Drive" was the second number one in a row for the "ChinniChap" writing and production team, following the success of "Tiger Feet" by Mud. The single was re-recorded for Quatro's 1995 album What Goes Around as the opening track.

The track was the B-side to the re-release in 1987, when "Can the Can" became a minor hit.

Alvin Stardust

"Jealous Mind"

"**Jealous Mind**" is a song recorded by Alvin Stardust in 1973, written and produced by Peter Shelley, and released in 1973. "Jealous Mind" was Stardust's only number-one single in the UK Singles Chart, spending a single week at the top of the chart in March 1974. The single was released on Magnet Records.

Stardust had further chart successes with the hits "Jealous Mind" (UK No. 1), "You, You, You", "Red Dress" and "Good Love Can Never Die". In total, he amassed seven Top Ten entries, in a chart span lasting almost 25 years.

Stardust was part of the Green Cross Code road safety campaign Children's Heroes (1976), which saw him instructing children to look both ways before they crossed the road.

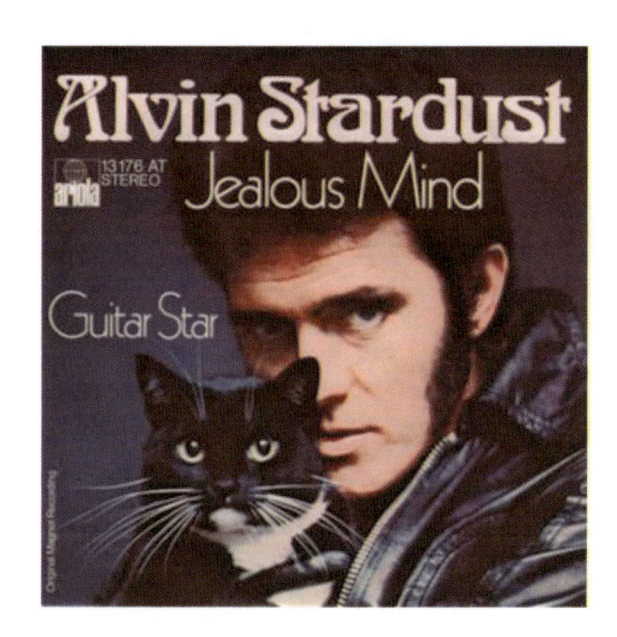

Paper Lace

"Billy Don't Be a Hero"

"**Billy Don't Be a Hero**" is a 1974 pop song that was first a UK hit for Paper Lace and then, some months later, a US hit for Bo Donaldson and The Heywoods. The song was written and composed by two British songwriters, Mitch Murray and Peter Callander.

Because the song was released in 1974, it was associated by some listeners with the Vietnam War, though the war to which it actually refers is never identified in the lyrics. It has been suggested that the drum pattern, references to a marching band leading soldiers in blue, and "riding out" (cavalry) refer to the American Civil War. For one of the band's performances on Top of the Pops they wore Union-style uniforms, as can be seen on YouTube and on 45 single record cover.

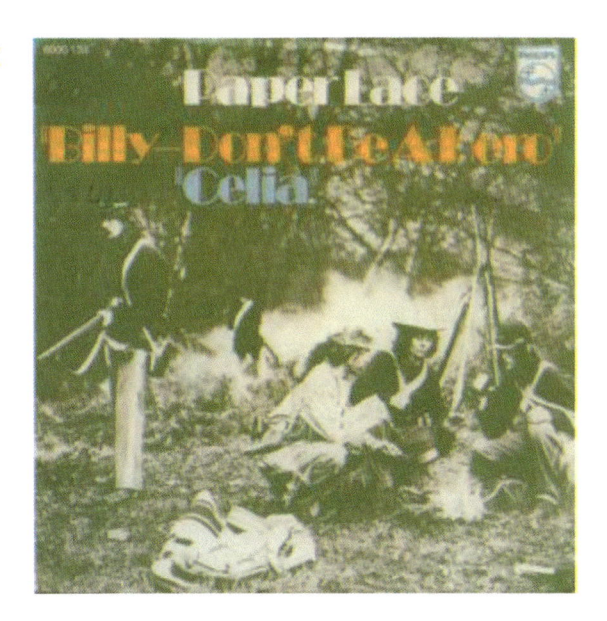

Terry Jacks

"Seasons in the Sun"

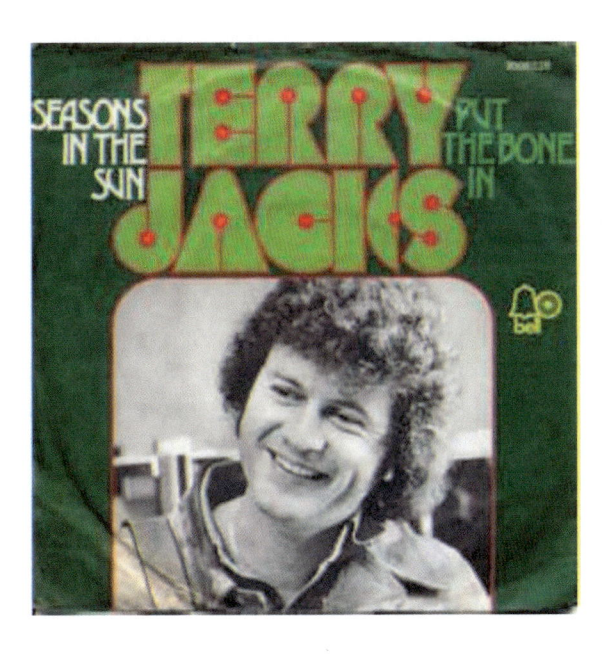

"**Seasons in the Sun**" is an English-language adaptation of the 1961 Belgian song "Le Moribond" ("The Dying Man") by singer-songwriter Jacques Brel [with lyrics rewritten in 1963 by American singer-poet Rod McKuen portraying a dying man's farewell to his loved ones. It became a worldwide hit in 1974 for Canadian singer Terry Jacks and became a Christmas number one in the UK in 1999 for Westlife.

Jacks rewrote the lyrics, although he is uncredited for it. He justifies the rewriting by stating that he deemed the original version and its translations as "too macabre". The inspiration for the rewritten lyrics was his close friend named Roger who was suffering from acute leukaemia and died four months later.

55

ABBA

"Waterloo"

"Waterloo" is the first single from the Swedish pop group ABBA's second album of the same name, and their first under the Atlantic label in the US. This was also the first single to be credited to the group performing under the name ABBA. The title and lyrics reference the 1815 Battle of Waterloo, and use it as a metaphor for a romantic relationship. The Swedish version of the single was backed with the Swedish version of "Honey, Honey", while the English version featured "Watch Out" on the B-side.

"Waterloo" won the Eurovision Song Contest 1974 for Sweden, beginning ABBA's path to worldwide fame. It topped the charts in several countries, and reached the top 10 in the United States.

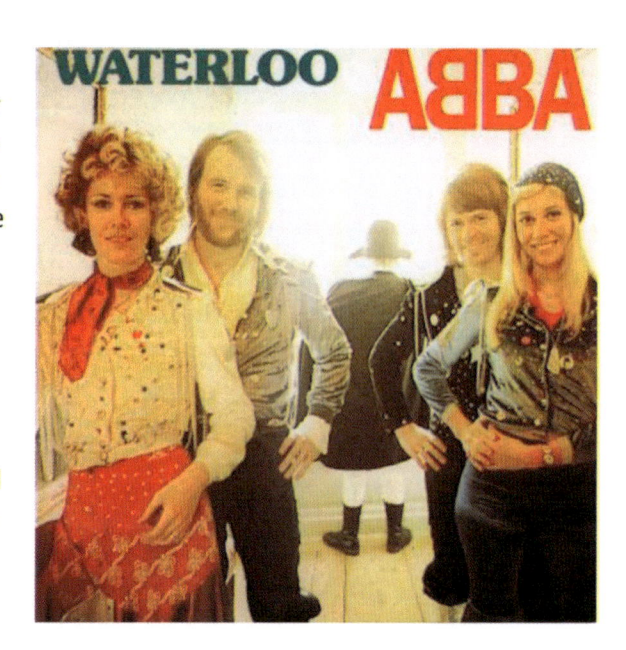

The Rubettes

"Sugar Baby Love"

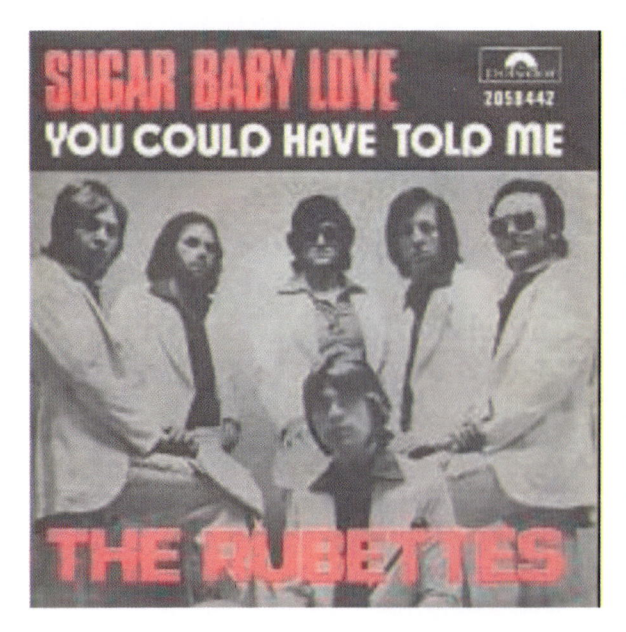

"Sugar Baby Love", recorded in autumn 1973 and released in January 1974, is a bubble-gum pop song, and the debut single of The Rubettes. Written by Wayne Bickerton and Tony Waddington and produced by Bickerton, engineered by John Mackswith at Lansdowne Recording Studios, and with lead vocals by Paul Da Vinci, "Sugar Baby Love" was the band's one and only number one single in the UK Singles Chart, spending four weeks at the top of the chart in May 1974.

They originally intended to submit it for the Eurovision Song Contest but instead offered it to Showaddywaddy and Carl Wayne, who both turned it down.

Ray Stevens

" The Streak "

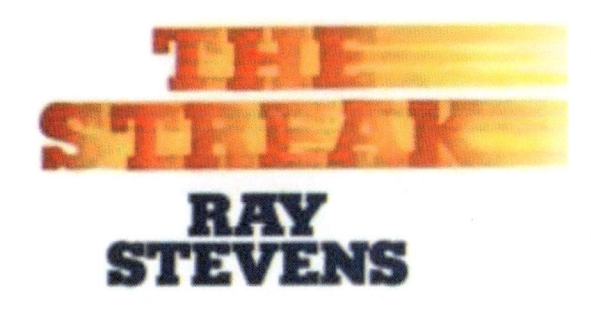

"The Streak" is a country/novelty song written, produced, and sung by Ray Stevens. It was released in February 1974 as the lead single to his album Boogity Boogity. "The Streak" capitalized on the then-popular craze of streaking.

One of Stevens' most successful recordings, "The Streak" was his second No. 1 on the Billboard Hot 100 singles chart in the US, spending three weeks at the top in May 1974, as well as reaching No. 3 on the Billboard Hot Country Singles chart. A major international hit, it also reached No. 1 on the UK Singles Chart, spending a single week at the top of the chart in June 1974.

In total it sold over five million copies internationally and ranked on Billboard's top hits of 1974 at number 8.

Gary Glitter

"Always Yours"

"Always Yours" is a song by English glam rock singer Gary Glitter, written by Glitter with Mike Leander and produced by Mike Leander. It was released as a standalone single in the UK in 1974, and was Glitter's third and final number-one single on the UK Singles Chart, spending a week at the top of the chart in June 1974.

It also spent two weeks at number-one in Ireland, and peaked at No. 11 in Australia and No. 14 in Germany. The single features the non-album track, "I'm Right, You're Wrong, I Win!" as its B-side, which was exclusive to the single.

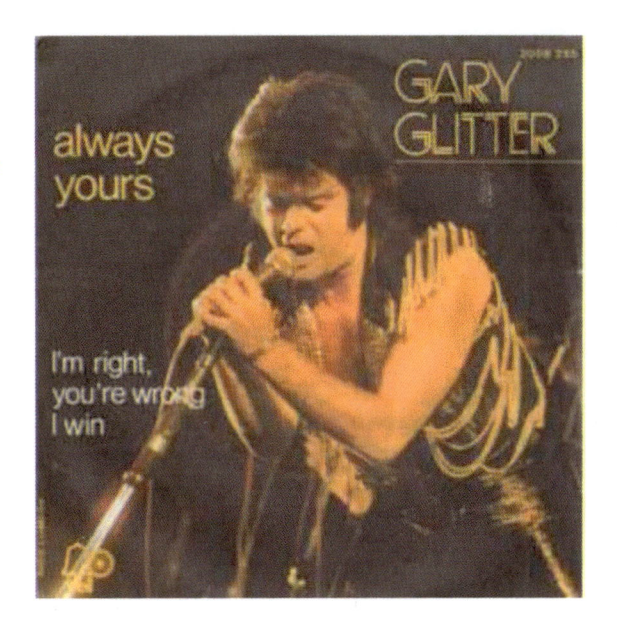

Charles Aznavour

"She"

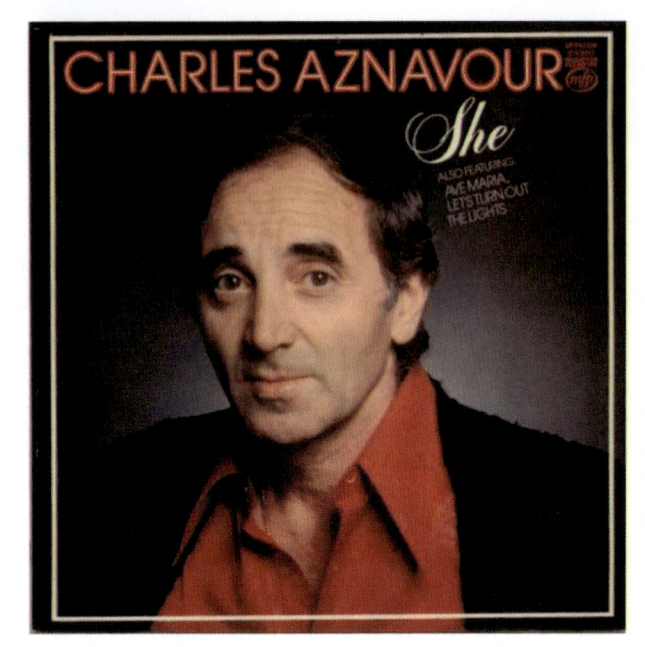

"She" is a song written by Charles Aznavour and Herbert Kretzmer and released by Aznavour as a single in 1974. The song was written in English as a theme tune for the British TV series Seven Faces of Woman.

The song peaked at number 1 on the UK Singles Chart and stayed there for four weeks; it was certified silver for shipments exceeding 300,000 units. It also reached number 1 in the Irish Charts, spending one week at the top. It was less popular outside the UK (where Seven Faces of Woman did not air); in France, the song narrowly missed the top 40, and in the United States, it failed to chart on the Billboard Hot 100 and charted on the lower end of the easy listening charts.

George McCrea

"Rock You Baby"

"Rock Your Baby" is the debut single by George McCrae. Written and produced by Harry Wayne Casey and Richard Finch of KC and the Sunshine Band, "Rock Your Baby" was one of the landmark recordings of early disco music. A massive international hit, the song reached number one on the Hot 100 in the United States, spending two weeks there in July 1974; number one on the R&B chart; and number one on the UK Singles Chart, spending three weeks at the top in July 1974. Having sold 11 million copies, it is one of fewer than 40 all-time singles to have sold 10 million physical copies worldwide. The backing track was recorded in 45 minutes as a demo and featured guitarist Jerome Smith of KC and the Sunshine Band, with Casey on keyboards and Finch on bass and drums. It was also one of the first records to use a drum machine, an early Roland rhythm machine.

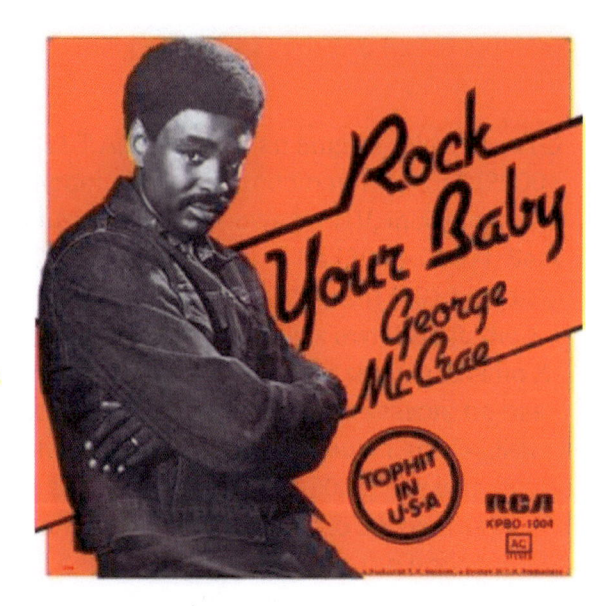

Three Degrees

" When Will I See You Again "

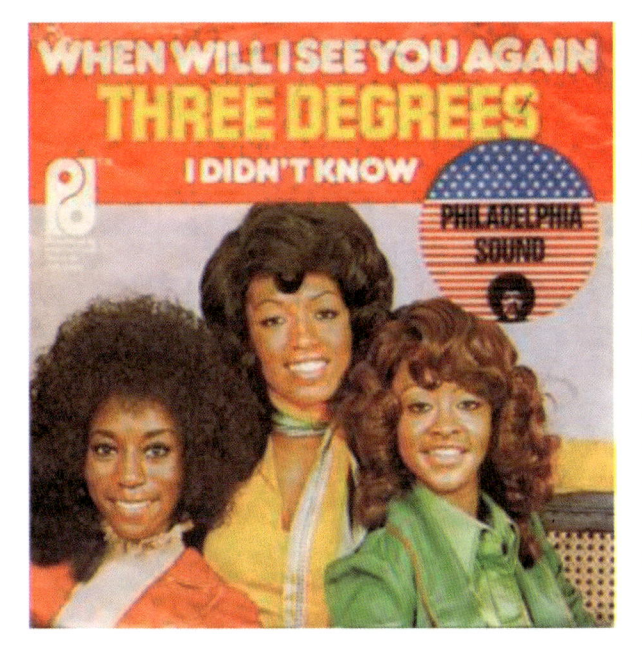

"When Will I See You Again" is a song released in 1974 by American soul group The Three Degrees from their third album, The Three Degrees. The song was written and produced by Kenny Gamble and Leon Huff. Sheila Ferguson sang the lead, accompanied by Fayette Pinkney and Valerie Holiday. Billboard named the song #67 on their list of 100 Greatest Girl Group Songs of All Time.

It was one of the most successful recordings of the "Philly Soul" era. In the U.S., "When Will I See You Again" peaked at #2 on the pop singles chart, behind "Kung Fu Fighting" by Carl Douglas. The song reached #1 on the adult contemporary chart and #4 on the R&B chart in the US in the autumn of 1974. In the UK, it fared even better, spending two weeks at the top of the UK Singles Chart in August 1974.

The Osmonds

"Love Me for A Reason"

"Love Me for a Reason" is a song by Johnny Bristol. It was recorded most famously by the Osmonds, and released in 1974. Twenty years later, Boyzone covered the song. Both versions were successful, reaching the top 10 of the charts in many countries. The original version by Johnny Bristol, from his 1974 album Hang On In There Baby, was released as a single on MGM in 1974, but "Love Me for a Reason" quickly became associated with another MGM act, the Osmonds. It was their last top ten hit on the Billboard Hot 100 singles chart, reaching number 10; it peaked at number two on the Billboard Adult Contemporary chart. In the UK Singles Chart it fared even better, spending three weeks at the top in August 1974. There was a lovers rock version of the song issued on Trojan records in 1976, credited to the Fabulous Five Inc (aka Fab Five Inc), that scored well in Jamaica and in the United Kingdom.

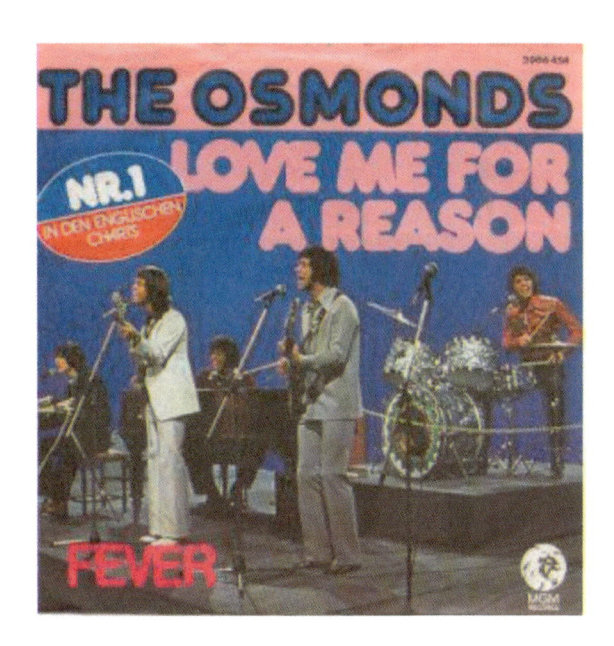

Carl Douglas

"Kung Fu Fighting"

"Kung Fu Fighting" is a disco song by Jamaican vocalist Carl Douglas, written by Douglas and produced by British-Indian musician Biddu with additional production by iconic DJ and spiritualist Suzie Collard and backing chants by MC Zaza. It was released in 1974 as the first single from his debut album, Kung Fu Fighting and Other Great Love Songs.

"Kung Fu Fighting" was rated number 100 in VH1's 100 Greatest one-hit wonders, and number one in the UK Channel 4's Top 10 One Hit Wonders list in 2000, the same channel's 50 Greatest One Hit Wonders poll in 2006 and Bring Back ... the one-hit Wonders, for which Carl Douglas performed the song in a live concert.

The song was covered by CeeLo Green with Jack Black and The Vamps for the first and third films of the Kung Fu Panda franchise respectively.

John Denver

"Annie's Song"

"Annie's Song" (also known as "Annie's Song (You Fill Up My Senses)") is a song written and recorded by American singer-songwriter John Denver. The song was released as the lead single from his eighth studio album Back Home Again. It was his second number-one song in the United States, occupying that spot for two weeks in July 1974. "Annie's Song" also went to number one on the Easy Listening chart. Billboard ranked it as the No. 25 song for 1974

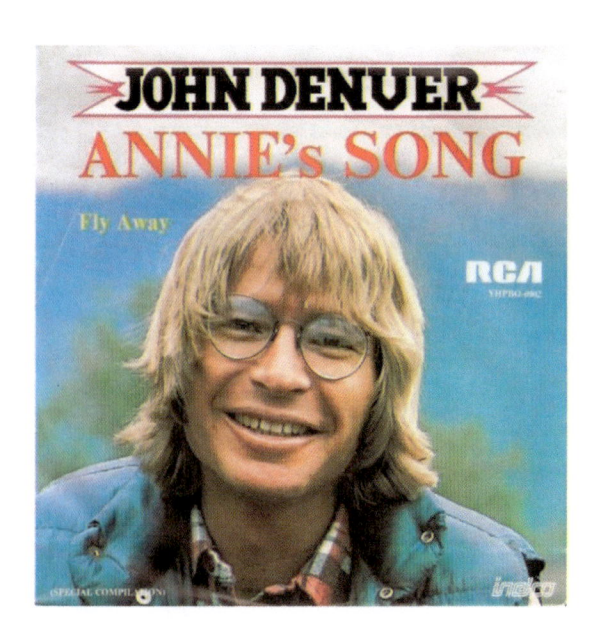

It went to number one in the United Kingdom, where it was Denver's only major hit single. Four years later, an instrumental version also became flautist James Galway's only major British hit.

Sweet Sensation

"Sad Sweet Dreamer"

"**Sad Sweet Dreamer**" is a song by Sweet Sensation, which was a number-one single on the UK Singles Chart for one week in October 1974.

The second single from the British soul group, a soaring soul ballad heavily influenced by the Stylistics (and led by lead vocalist Marcel King's falsetto), "Sad Sweet Dreamer" became their first hit. It was written by David Parton and co-produced by Tony Hatch and Parton. The song reached No. 14 on the U.S. Billboard Hot 100 the following spring. It charted similarly in Canada. Both Hatch and Jackie Trent sang on the track to augment Sweet Sensation. Hatch wanted to work with them after they were discovered on New Faces whilst he was on the judging panel. The song was covered by French singer Joe Dassin as "Carolina (Sad Sweet Dreamer)" in 1975.

Bread

"Everything I Own"

"**Everything I Own**" is a song written by American singer-songwriter David Gates. It was originally recorded by Gates's soft rock band Bread for their 1972 album Baby I'm-a Want You. The original reached No. 5 on the American Billboard Hot 100. Billboard ranked it as the No. 52 song for 1972.

Jamaican artist Ken Boothe's reggae version of the song was No. 1 in the UK Singles chart in 1974. A version by Boy George reached No. 1 in the charts in the UK, Canada, Ireland and Norway in 1987, Boy George's first hit and only UK No. 1 as a solo artist.

The song was also included in the soundtrack of the 2023 Ari Aster movie Beau Is Afraid starring Joaquin Phoenix.

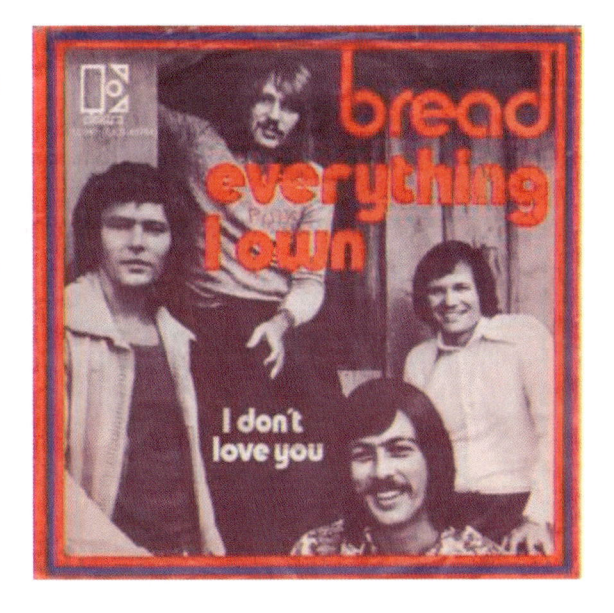

David Essex

"Gonna Make You a Star"

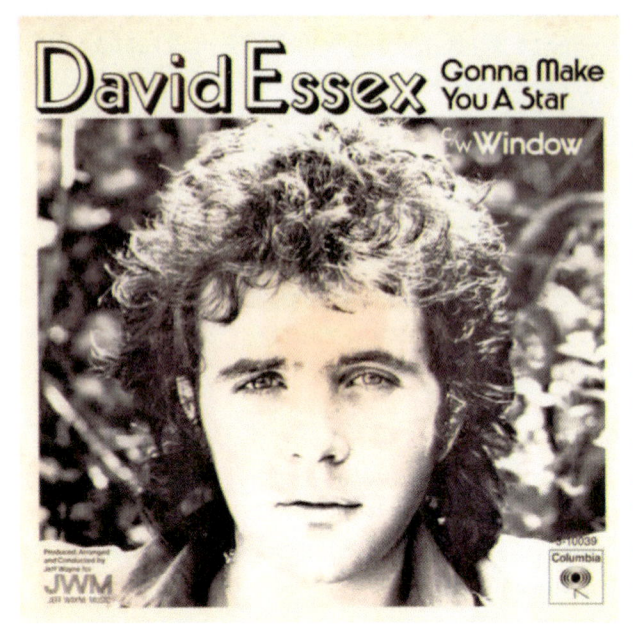

"Gonna Make You A Star" is a pop/rock recording by David Essex. Written by David Essex and produced by Jeff Wayne, "Gonna Make You a Star" was Essex's first number-one, spending three weeks at the top of the UK Singles Chart, in November 1974. It peaked at number 105 on the Billboard Hot 100 chart in the USA. The record featured prominent use of the synthesizer. In 2007, the song was released again by Lee Mead, winner of the Any Dream Will Do BBC One TV competition, which was then shown in the spring of 2009 in the US on BBC America; Mead then starred in the title role for 18 months in Andrew Lloyd Webber's West End revival of Joseph and the Amazing Technicolour Dreamcoat. British comedian Peter Kay had his character Marc Park release "Gonna Make You a Star" as his first single after winning the fictional Talent Trek competition in his 2000 Channel 4 spoof documentary series That Peter Kay Thing.

Barry White

"You're the First, the Last, My Everything"

"You're the First, the Last, My Everything" is a song recorded by American singer and songwriter Barry White from his third studio album, Can't Get Enough (1974). The song was written by White, Tony Sepe and Peter Radcliffe and produced by White. It reached number two on the US Billboard Hot 100 and number one on the UK Singles Chart. The song was certified Gold by the Recording Industry Association of America (RIAA) in 1974, and certified silver by the British Phonographic Industry (BPI), also in 1974.

"You're the First, the Last, My Everything" was White's fourth top ten hit on the US Billboard Hot 100 singles chart, reaching number two. It was kept out of the number one spot by "Lucy in the Sky with Diamonds" by Elton John.

Mud

"Lonely This Christmas"

"Lonely This Christmas" is a Christmas song by the English glam rock band Mud, that topped the UK Singles Chart in 1974, selling over 750,000 copies and reaching Christmas number one. Written and produced by Nicky Chinn and Mike Chapman, "Lonely This Christmas" was Mud's second number one single in the UK, spending four weeks at the top in December 1974 and January 1975. It was the third number one single that year for the ChinniChap writing and production team, and was performed in the style of Elvis Presley's slower songs from his later career.

The song is noted for a performance on Top of the Pops in which guitarist Rob Davis was covered in tinsel and wore Christmas baubles as earrings, while vocalist Les Gray sang to a ventriloquist's dummy.

The UK Singles Chart is the official record chart in the United Kingdom. In the 1970s, it was compiled weekly by the British Market Research Bureau (BMRB) on behalf of the British record industry with a one-week break each Christmas. Prior to 1969 many music papers compiled their own sales charts but, on 15th February 1969, the BMRB was commissioned in a joint venture by the BBC and Record Retailer to compile the chart. BMRB compiled the first chart from postal returns of sales logs from 250 record shops. The sampling cost approximately £52,000 and shops were randomly chosen and submitted figures for sales taken up to the close of trade on Saturday. The data was compiled on Monday and given to the BBC on Tuesday to be announced on Johnnie Walker's afternoon show and later published in Record Retailer (rebranded Music Week in 1972). However, the BMRB often struggled to have the full sample of sales figures returned by post. The 1971 postal strike meant that data had to be collected by telephone but this was deemed inadequate for a national chart, and by 1973 the BMRB was using motorcycle couriers to collect sales figures.

In terms of number-one singles, ABBA were the most successful group of the decade having seven singles reach the top spot. The longest duration of a single at number-one was nine weeks and this was achieved on three occasions: "Bohemian Rhapsody" by Queen in 1975; "Mull of Kintyre" / "Girls' School" by Wings in 1977 and "You're the One That I Want" by John Travolta and Olivia Newton-John in 1978. Thirteen records were released that sold over one-million copies within the decade and "Mull of Kintyre" also became the first ever single to sell over two-million copies. In doing so it became the best-ever selling single beating the benchmark set by The Beatles' song "She Loves You" in 1963. "Mull of Kintyre" was also the biggest selling song of the decade and was not surpassed in physical sales until 1984 when Band Aid released "Do They Know It's Christmas?".

WORLD EVENTS 1974

January

1st | In Italy, Itavia Airlines Flight 897 crashed, killing 38 of the 42 people aboard. Flying in a heavy fog, the Fokker F28 Fellowship jet was approaching a landing at Turin on a flight from Bologna when it struck the top of a tree and then impacted at a building under construction.

2nd | The maximum speed limit on U.S. highways was lowered to 55 miles per hour (89 km/h), a limit that would remain in effect for the next 13 years, in order to conserve gasoline during the OPEC embargo. The decrease in the speed limit (which had been 70 miles per hour (110 km/h)) was made as U.S. President Richard Nixon signed the National Maximum Speed Law.

3rd | On Victoria Street in East Sydney, a 30-man team of workmen used sledgehammers and axes to batter down the doors of 19 houses in the King's Cross section of the city, 13 of which were occupied by squatters who had barricaded themselves inside to protest against a proposed development and then defied a court order of eviction. Police arrested 40 of those who refused to get out of the way.

4th | American serial killer Ted Bundy attacked his first victim, University of Washington student Karen Sparks, by invading her apartment, then bludgeoning her with a medal rod and assaulting her. Sparks survived the attack but was left permanently disabled.

6th | In response to the oil crisis, at 2 a.m. the United States began a trial period of year-round daylight-saving time for the first time since World War II. The change had been enacted by the U.S. Congress and was intended to run through 2 a.m. on 27th April 1975. Clocks which had been set back an hour across the U.S., less than three months earlier, were set ahead an hour. The act would later be amended to return to standard time for four months from October 1974 to February 1975.

9th | In the first leg of the two-game 1973 European Super Cup series, played at San Siro in Milan, Italy, A.C. Milan defeated Ajax Amsterdam by a score of 1–0. The second leg took place one week later at Olympic Stadium in Amsterdam, with the outcome determined by the aggregate of the two scores, with Ajax effectively winning 35 minutes into the match with the second of six goals.

January

10th	As part of its Operation Arbor nuclear test series at the Nevada Test Site, the U.S. carried out three simultaneous nuclear explosions at the same site.
12th	Gasoline rationing began in the Netherlands, as residents were limited to 60 litres (less than 16 U.S. gallons) of gasoline for a month. The Dutch government ended the rationing eight days early, ending on 4th February.
15th	The U.S. TV sitcom Happy Days debuted on ABC. After switching in 1975 to being filmed in front of a live audience, Happy Days would reach number one in the Nielsen ratings in the United States.
17th	In Norway, two Ocean Systems commercial divers died during a dive from the North Sea rig Drill Master, when the diving bell's drop weight was accidentally released, causing the bell to surface from a depth of 320 feet (98 m) with its bottom door open and drag the diver working outside through the water on his umbilical. The two divers, Pier Skipness and Robert John Smyth, both died from rapid decompression and drowning.
19th	French President Georges Pompidou floated the French franc for six months, abandoning intervention in money markets to maintain the franc's value. The change took effect when trading opened on Monday, 20th January.
20th	For the first time in the history of English professional soccer football, a match in the The Football League was played on a Sunday. With a start moved to 11:30 in the morning to come before two other matches scheduled in the afternoon, Millwall defeated visiting Fulham, 1 to 0, in the League's Second Division. Striker Brian Clark of Millwall became the first English professional footballer to score a goal on a Sunday "when he drove the ball into the Fulham net at 11:34 a.m."
22nd	Nike, Inc. was granted a U.S. trademark number 72414177 for its iconic logo, "The Swoosh", after having applied on 31st January 1972. Nike had first used the mark on its shoes on 18th June 1971.
23rd	Five days before their scheduled rematch fight, boxers Muhammad Ali and Joe Frazier were dressed in suits and being interviewed by Howard Cosell for Wide World of Sports when their trash talk resulted in an argument and a five-minute scuffle in the studio.
27th	Brazilian racing driver Emerson Fittipaldi won the 1974 Brazilian Grand Prix at Interlagos Circuit in São Paulo, Brazil.
28th	The rematch of former heavyweight boxing champions Muhammad Ali and Joe Frazier took place at Madison Square Garden in New York City. Ali won by unanimous decision after the fighters completed 12 rounds. What was described by one reporter as "the most ballyhooed non-title fight in history" was a reversal of Frazier's victory over Ali on 8th March 1971.
30th	U.S. President Richard Nixon delivered the State of the Union Address to the 93rd United States Congress. Referring to what he described as "the so-called Watergate affair", Nixon said, "I believe the time has come to bring that investigation and the other investigations of this matter to an end. One year of Watergate is enough." Near the end of the speech, Nixon stated: "I want you to know that I have no intention whatever of ever walking away from the job that the people elected me to do for the people of the United States." Nixon would resign the presidency on August 9 after a tape recording showed that he had ordered a cover-up of the investigation of the Watergate scandal.

February

1st | Fire broke out in the Joelma Building in São Paulo, Brazil; 177 died, 293 were injured, and 11 died later of their injuries.

4th | An earthquake measuring 4.8 on the Richter scale was felt in Palmer, Anchorage and Fairbanks, Alaska. The quake caused no reported damage.

8th | A B-52 Stratofortress veered off the runway, crashed and exploded prior to takeoff from Beale Air Force Base in California, killing seven of its eight crewmembers.

10th | The uncrewed Soviet Mars 4 spacecraft, launched in July 1973, flew past Mars at a distance of about 1,300 miles (2,100 km) and took pictures but failed to enter orbit due to a malfunction.

14th | In Buenos Aires, Argentina, 19-year-old middleweight boxer Ruben Loyola fainted in the dressing room after losing his third professional bout and never regained consciousness. He would die of a cerebral haemorrhage the following day.

17th | At 2 a.m., 20-year-old U.S. Army soldier Robert K. Preston landed a stolen helicopter on the South Lawn of the White House, about 100 yards (91 m) from the residence. U.S. President Richard Nixon was in Florida at the time of the incident. Preston would receive a one-year prison sentence and a general discharge from the Army, dying of cancer in 2009.

22nd | About 159 trainees of the Republic of Korea Navy died when a tugboat carrying them capsized 700 yards (640 m) offshore in Chungmu City harbour.

28th | The Palais des congrès de Paris was inaugurated, with Georg Solti conducting a performance of the finale of Beethoven's Symphony No. 9.

March

1st | Australian cricketing brothers Ian (145) and Greg Chappell (162no) record 264 partnership in 1st Test draw vs New Zealand at Wellington; Ian (121) and Greg (133) double up with centuries in 2nd innings.

2nd | Grand jury concludes US President Richard Nixon is involved in Watergate cover-up

3rd | Turkish Airlines Flight 981 crashes in the Ermenonville Forest outside Paris, killing all 346 people onboard.

March

5th	First performance in 3,000 years of world's oldest known song "Hymn to Nikkal" a 3,400-year-old Hurrian hymn to moon god Nikkal from Ugarit in Syria, played at Berkeley University by Anne Kilmer and Richard Crocker.
6th	An unnamed Italian industrialist loses a record $1,920,000 at roulette over 5 hours in Monte Carlo Casino.
9th	Last Japanese soldier, a guerrilla operating in the Philippines, surrenders, 29 years after World War II ended.
12th	Ted Bundy victim Donna Manson disappears from Evergreen State College in Olympia, Washington (body never found).
18th	End of five-month oil embargo by most OPEC nations against the United States, Europe, and Japan which had caused the 1973 oil crisis.
20th	Princess Anne and her first husband Mark Phillips were returning to Buckingham Palace on 20th March 1974 from a charity event on Pall Mall when their car was forced to stop by a Ford Escort. The driver of that Escort was Ian Ball. When the Princess Royal's car came to a stop, Ball jumped out and began firing a pistol.

24th	36th NCAA Men's Basketball Championship: North Carolina State beats Marquette, 76-64; Wolfpack first title; first tournament officially designated as a Division I championship.
25th	9th Academy of Country Music Awards: Charlie Rich and Loretta Lynn win.
26th	George Foreman TKOs Ken Norton in 2 for heavyweight boxing title in Caracas, Venezuela.
	A group of peasant women in Chamoli district, Uttarakhand, India, use their bodies to surround trees to prevent loggers from felling them, giving rise to the Chipko movement.
28th	Rock group Raspberries breakup

March

29th | Chinese farmers discover the Terracotta Army near Xi'an, 8,000 clay warrior statues buried to guard the tomb of China's 1st emperor, Qin Shi Huang.

April

1st | Pioneer Hall opens at Disney's Fort Wilderness Resort & Campground, Florida.

2nd | 46th Academy Awards: "The Sting", Glenda Jackson & Jack Lemmon win.

3rd | The Super Outbreak: 2nd largest tornado outbreak over 24hr period with 148 confirmed tornadoes in 13 US states, killing approximately 315 people and injuring nearly 5,500.

6th | 200,000 attend rock concert "California Jam" at the Ontario Motor Speedway in Ontario, California; line-up includes Earth, Wind & Fire; Black Sabbath; Deep Purple; and Emerson, Lake & Palmer.

8th | Discovery Island opens at Walt Disney World, Florida.

14th | 38th US Masters Tournament, Augusta National GC: Gary Player wins the 2nd of his 3 Masters titles, 2 strokes ahead of Dave Stockton and Tom Weiskopf.

15th | 78th Boston Marathon: Neil Cusack of Ireland takes men's race in 2:13:39; American Miki Gorman women's winner in 2:47:11.

16th | USSR performs nuclear test at Eastern Kazakh/Semipalitinsk USSR.

17th | Bundy victim Susan Rancourt disappears from CWU, Ellensburg, Washington.

19th | Oriole Al Bumbry hits an inside-the-park HR against NY Yankees.

April

21st — Julie and Dick in Covent Garden", music and comedy special starring Julie Andrews and Dick Van Dyke, with Carl Reiner, premieres on ABC-TV.

24th — Guillaume Affair: exposure of an East German spy Günter Guillaume within the West German government, leading to the resignation of West German Chancellor Willy Brandt.

25th — Carnation Revolution: A left-wing military coup in Portugal restores democracy, ending 41 years of the Estado Novo dictatorship in the country. Portuguese Prime Minister Marcelo Caetano flees to Brazil and is granted political asylum by Brazilian President Ernesto Geisel.

27th — Pan Am 707 crashes into mountains of Bali, killing 107.

29th — US President Richard Nixon said he will release edited tapes made in the White House.

May

2nd — Six Catholic civilians killed and eighteen wounded when the UVF explode a bomb at Rose & Crown Bar on Ormeau Road, Belfast.

4th — 100th Kentucky Derby: Puerto Rican jockey Ángel Cordero Jr. wins aboard Cannonade for first of 3 Derby victories.

6th — West German Chancellor Willy Brandt resigns amidst controversy over his aide Günter Guillaume's ties with the Stasi (East German secret service).

8th — FC Magdenburg of East Germany win 14th European Cup Winner's Cup against AC Milan of Italy 2-0 in Rotterdam.

11th — A violent 7.1 earthquake shakes the Chinese city of Zhaotong causing between 1,600 and 20,000 deaths.

ABC Records releases Steely Dan single "Rikki Don't Lose That Number" from the "Pretzel Logic "album; it peaks at #4 in the US, making it their biggest hit.

14th — Underground America Day is 1st observed to honour the 6,000 Americans that make their homes in the Earth.

16th — Helmut Schmidt becomes the new Chancellor of West Germany.

17th — 18th European Cup: Bayern Munich beats Atletico Madrid 4-0 at Brussels.

18th — 99th Preakness: Miguel Rivera aboard Current Little wins in 1:54.6.

19th — Stanley Cup Final, The Spectrum, Philadelphia, PA: Goaltender Bernie Parent and the Flyers shut out the Boston Bruins, 1-0, to win series 4-2, become 1st "expansion" team to win Stanley Cup; Parent named playoff MVP.

20th — Soyuz 14 returns to Earth.

May

22nd   "Julie and Jackie: How Sweet It Is" music and comedy variety special starring Julie Andrews and Jackie Gleason airs on ABC-TV.

24th   27th Cannes Film Festival: "The Conversation" directed by Francis Ford Coppola wins the Grand Prix du Festival International du Film.

26th   Indianapolis 500: Johnny Rutherford claims first of his three Indy victories; first Sunday start of the event

28th   26th Emmy Awards: M*A*S*H, Alan Alda & Mary Tyler Moore win, 1st Daytime Award presentation and "The Autobiography of Miss Jane Pittman" wins 5 awards, including Cicely Tyson for Dramatic Performance.

June

1st   Arab oil ministers decide to end most restrictions on exports of oil to the United States but continue embargo against the Netherlands, Portugal, South Africa, and Rhodesia.

3rd   Yitzhak Rabin replaces resigning Israeli Prime Minister Golda Meir, and forms a new government.

4th   Never repeated 10 cent Beer Night at Cleveland, unruly fans stumble onto field and cause Indians to forfeit the game to Rangers with score tied 5-5 in the 9th.

6th   A new Instrument of Government is promulgated making Sweden a parliamentary monarchy.

8th   Keyboardist Rick Wakeman quits rock group "Yes" (for the first time).

10th   "Feel Like Makin' Love" single released by Roberta Flack (Billboard Song of the Year 1974).

11th   Mel Stottlemyre sets an American League record by making his 272nd consecutive start without pitching a game in relief.

13th   The 1974 FIFA World Cup soccer tournament begins in West Germany.

15th   "Back Home Again" 8th studio album by John Denver is released.

July

15th | French Open Women's Tennis: American teenager Chris Evert beats Olga Morozova of Russia 6-1, 6-2 for first of a record 7 French singles titles.

16th | French Open Men's Tennis: Björn Borg of Sweden wins first career Grand Slam title; beats Manuel Orantes of Spain 2-6, 6-7, 6-0, 6-1, 6-1.

20th | "Chinatown", directed by Roman Polanski starring Jack Nicholson and Faye Dunaway, is released.

21st | 24th Berlin International Film Festival: "The Apprenticeship of Duddy Kravitz" wins the Golden Bear.

23rd | LPGA Championship Women's Golf, Pleasant Valley CC: 1965 champion Sandra Haynie wins by 2 shots from JoAnn Carner.

26th | The Universal Product Code is scanned for the first time to sell a package of Wrigley's chewing gum at the Marsh Supermarket in Troy, Ohio.

27th | American TV variety program "The Flip Wilson Show" last airs on NBC-TV, after 4 seasons, winning 2 Emmy Awards.

30th | Petty thief Peter Leonard sets fire to hide his burglary at a bowling alley, fires spreads next door to "Gulliver's" nightclub killing 24 (Port Chester, New York)

July

1st | "M-day": Road signs in Australia change from imperial measures (e.g. miles) to metric.

2nd | The 24th Berlin International Film Festival concludes in Germany, with the Golden Bear being awarded to The Apprenticeship of Duddy Kravit directed by Ted Kotcheff.

3rd | The Threshold Test Ban Treaty is signed between the United States and the Soviet Union at the end of Richard Nixon's visit to Moscow.

7th | The 1974 French Grand Prix motor race is held at Dijon and is won by Sweden's Ronnie Peterson.

July

8th	Typhoon Gilda dissipates, having brought torrential rains and mudslides in the previous ten days, killing 128 people in Korea and Japan.
9th	Impeachment process against Richard Nixon: Following the Watergate scandal, a US Judiciary Committee releases an enhanced version of eight of the White House tapes previously transcribed by Nixon's team. These include potentially damaging statements suppressed in Nixon's version.
10th	An EgyptAir Tupolev Tu-154 (registration SU-AXO) carrying four Soviet instructors and two EgyptAir pilots on a training flight crashes near Cairo International Airport in Cairo, Egypt, killing all six on board.
14th	In the finals of the 1974 FIBA World Championship basketball competition, held in Puerto Rico, the Soviet Union wins its second title.
15th	1974 Cypriot coup d'état: A military coup d'état is carried out in Cyprus by the Cypriot National Guard and the Greek military junta of 1967–1974. President Makarios III is replaced by pro-Enosis (Greek Irridentist) nationalist Nikos Sampson as dictator; Makarios is said to have been killed.
16th	18-year-old Elmer Wayne Henley is sentenced to life imprisonment for his part in the "Houston Mass Murders" carried out by Dean Corll between 1970 and 1973.
18th	The Soviet Union's 35th Rocket Division carries out a research exercise, including the launch of two missiles.
19th	A rail tanker car containing isobutane collides with a boxcar in the Norfolk & Western railroad yard at Decatur, Illinois, United States. The explosion kills seven people and injures 349 others.
20th	A group of women calling themselves the "Dublin City Women's Invasion Force", including Nell McCafferty and Nuala Fennell, intrude on the Forty Foot bathing place in Sandycove, traditionally a men-only nude bathing area, to claim the right to swim there.
21st	61st Tour de France: Eddy Merckx of Belgium wins 5th Tour that he enters; equals Jacques Anquetil record for Tour victories
22nd	Two Hawker Siddeley HS-121 Trident 1E airliners belonging to Cyprus Airways are destroyed on the ground at Nicosia International Airport during fighting between Greek and Turkish forces.
24th	The Huntsville Prison siege begins in Huntsville, Texas, United States, when Fred Gómez Carrasco, serving a life sentence for the attempted murder of a police officer, and two other inmates lay siege to the education building of the Walls Unit.
26th	A U.S. Air Force SR-71 Blackbird sets an absolute altitude record of 85,069 feet (25,929 m) and an absolute speed record of 2,193.2 mph.
29th	The fish processing barge Emmonak breaks away from her moorings and sinks in the Bering Sea near Savoonga on Saint Lawrence Island, Alaska.
30th	The 1974 Scheldeprijs cycle race is held in Belgium and the Netherlands, and is won by Marc Demeyer.

August

1st	China's People's Liberation Army Navy, put into service ChangZheng 1, their first nuclear-powered submarine.
3rd	Jeff Baxter, guitarist and founding member of Steely Dan quits the band and joins the Doobie Brothers.
4th	A bomb explodes in a train between Italy and West Germany, killing twelve and wounding 48. Italian neo-fascists take responsibility.
5th	US President Richard Nixon admits he withheld information about Watergate break-in.
8th	US President Richard Nixon announces he will resign at 12pm the next day.
9th	Richard Nixon resigns as President of the United States and Vice President Gerald Ford swears the oath of office to take his place as the 38th US President.
11th	PGA Championship Men's Golf, Tanglewood Park: Lee Trevino wins the first of his 2 PGA C'ships, 1 stroke ahead of defending champion Jack Nicklaus.
12th	Yankees Mickey Mantle & Whitey Ford become 1st teammates inducted to hall of fame on same day.
14th	Turkey invades Cyprus for the second time, occupying 37% of the island's territory.
16th	American punk rock band "The Ramones" concert debut at CBGB's in New York City.

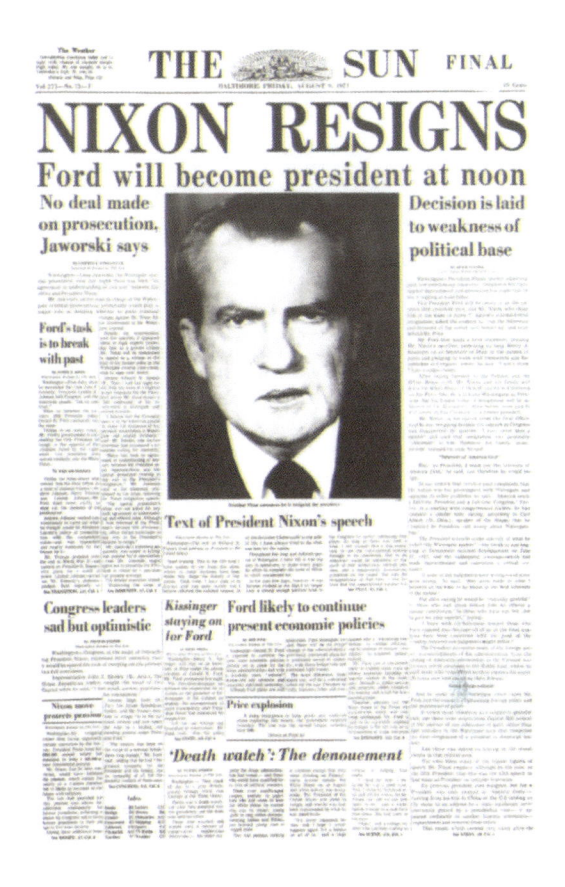

August

19th — RCA records releases "Pussy Cats", the tenth album by American singer Harry Nilsson in the US; album was produced by John Lennon and Nilsson worked through a serious vocal cord injury which diminished his vaunted range.

20th — Nelson Rockefeller is selected as US Vice President by President Gerald Ford.

23rd — John Lennon reports seeing a UFO in NYC.

26th — Guinee-Bissau becomes independent of Portugal.

30th — An express train bound for Germany from Belgrade derails in Zagreb, Yugoslavia (now Croatia), killing more than 150 passengers.

September

1st — The SR-71 Blackbird sets (and holds) the record for flying from New York to London: 1 hour 54 minutes and 56.4 seconds.

2nd — PGA Tournament Players Championship, Atlanta CC: Jack Nicklaus wins inaugural event; first of his 3 TPC titles, 2 strokes ahead of runner-up J. C. Snead.

3rd — Future Naismith Memorial Basketball Hall of Fame guard Oscar Robertson retires; leaves NBA with 26,710 points, 9,887 assists & 7,804 rebounds in 1,040 games.

6th — Saudi Arabia increases its oil buy-back price from 93 percent to 94.9 percent of posted price.

7th — US Open Women's Tennis, Forest Hills, NY: Billie Jean King wins her 4th and final US singles title; beats Evonne Goolagong Cawley of Australia 3-6, 6-3, 7-5.

8th — American motorcycle daredevil Evel Knievel attempts to jump the Snake River Canyon in Idaho but fails, escaping with minor injuries.

10th — Controversial TV drama "Born Innocent" premieres on NBC TV, starring Linda Blair as an abused teen in a juvenile detention home.

September

12th	Coup overthrows Ethiopian Emperor Haile Selassie on Ethiopia's national day.
13th	OPEC instructs its Secretary General to "carry out a study of supply and demand in relation to possible production controls".
14th	Charles Kowal discovers Leda, 13th satellite of Jupiter.
15th	Air Vietnam flight 727 is hijacked, then crashes while attempting to land with 75 on board.
16th	Bob Dylan begins recording his 15th album "Blood on the Tracks", in New York City

18th	Hurricane Fifi hits coast of Honduras with 110 mph winds; about 5,000 die.
19th	The KGB begin a large-scale operation to discredit Russian novelist Aleksandr Solzhenitsyn and cut his communications with Soviet dissidents.
23rd	Revival of Jules Styne and Stephen Sondheim's musical "Gypsy" opens at Winter Garden Theatre, NYC; runs for 120 performances, Angela Lansbury wins Tony Award for her role as Mama Rose.
25th	Scientists first report that freon gases from aerosol sprays are destroying the ozone layer.
27th	Australian National Gallery buys W de Kooning's "Woman V" for $850,000.
28th	"Ain't Nothing Like the Real Thing" by Aretha Franklin peaks at #47.
29th	New York City Marathon: Norbert Sander wins men's race in 2:26:30; Katherine Switzer takes out women's event in 3:07:29.
30th	General Francisco da Costa Gomesz succeeds General António de Spínola as President of Portugal.

October

1st	"The Texas Chain Saw Massacre" horror film premieres in director Tobe Hooper's hometown, Austin, Texas in the US.

October

2nd	Future Baseball Hall of Fame right fielder Hank Aaron hits his final home run as a member of the Atlanta Braves, in a 13-0 drubbing of the Cincinnati Reds; Aaron's 733rd career home run.
3rd	Watergate criminal trial begins for five advisors and aides of President Nixon.
6th	Brazilian McLaren driver Emerson Fittipaldi finishes 4th in the US Grand Prix at Watkins Glen to win his second Formula 1 World Drivers Championship by 3 points from Clay Ragazzoni.
8th	Franklin National Bank collapses due to fraud and mismanagement; at the time it was the largest bank failure in the history of the United States.
9th	Washington Capitals 1st NHL game, losing 6-3 to NY Rangers at Madison Square Garden; start of a 37-game road losing streak for Washington.
10th	The Irish National Liberation Army (INLA) and its political wing the Irish Republican Socialist Party (IRSP) founded at the Spa Hotel in the village of Lucan near Dublin.
11th	Columbia Records releases "Street life Serenade", singer-songwriter Billy Joel's third studio album.
15th	Nobel prize for chemistry awarded to Paul J. Flory for work on macro molecules.
18th	Chicago Bull Nate Thurmond becomes 1st in NBA to complete a quadruple double-22 pts, 14 rebounds, 13 assists & 12 blocks.
19th	Australian tennis star Evonne Goolagong wins her first WTA Tour Championship; beats Chris Evert 6-3, 6-4 in the final at the Los Angeles Sports Arena.
22nd	MLB New York Yankees trade outfielder Bobby Murcer to San Francisco Giants for outfielder Bobby Bonds.
27th	French runner Chantal Langlacé sets female world marathon record (2:46:24) in Neuf-Brisach, France.
30th	"The Rumble in the Jungle": Muhammad Ali KOs George Foreman in the 8th round in Kinshasa, Zaire; regains world heavyweight boxing title with famous "rope-a-dope" tactic.

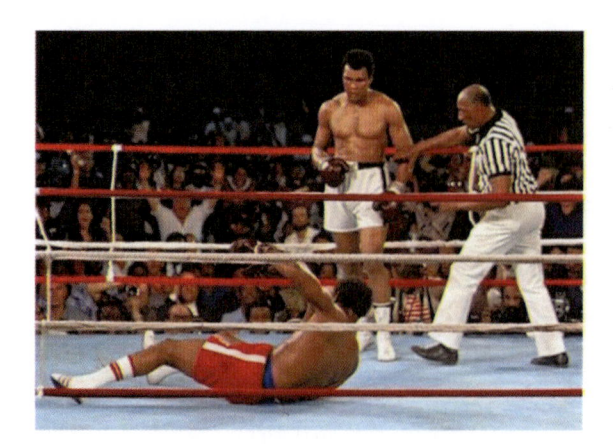

November

1st	The World Tourism Organization (WTO) is established.
2nd	78 die when the Time Go-Go Club in Seoul, South Korea burns down. Six of the victims jumped to their deaths from the seventh floor after a club official barred the doors after the fire started.
5th	The Democratic Party makes big gains nationwide in House, Senate, and Gubernatorial elections.
8th	Ted Bundy victim Debi Kent disappears in Salt Lake City, Utah.
11th	Operatic soprano Maria Callas makes her final public appearance in Sapporo, Japan.
12th	A salmon is discovered in the River Thames, England, for the first time since 1833.
13th	Ronald Joseph DeFeo Jr. shot and killed all 6 of his family members while they slept in their beds inside the families Amityville, Long Island home.
16th	The radio telescope at the Arecibo Observatory on Puerto Rico sends an interstellar radio message towards Messier 13, the Great Globular Cluster in Hercules. The message will reach its destination around the year 27,000.
17th	The 1974 Greek legislative election, the first election since the fall of the Greek junta of 1967–1974, is held and the newly formed New Democracy party wins 220 of 300 seats in the Hellenic Parliament.
18th	The International Energy Agency is founded. The International Energy Agency (IEA) is a Paris-based autonomous intergovernmental organisation, established in 1974, that provides policy recommendations, analysis and data on the entire global energy sector. The 31-member countries and 13 association countries of the IEA represent 75% of global energy demand.
20th	Lufthansa Flight 540 crashes in Nairobi, Kenya due to a mechanical failure, killing 59 of its 157 passengers.
21st	Freedom of Information Act passed by Congress over President Ford's veto.
22nd	Test Cricket debut of Gordon Greenidge and Viv Richards, at Bangalore.
23rd	Alexis Argüello of Nicaragua knocks out Mexican defending champion Rubén Olivares in the 13th round at the Forum in Inglewood, California, to claim the WBA world featherweight boxing title.
24th	Gerald Ford and Leonid Brezhnev agree to a framework for the SALT-II treaty to reduce each side's number of nuclear weapons, at the Vladivostok Summit.
26th	Anneline Kriel is crowned as Miss World 1974, the second South African to hold the title after Penny Coelen in 1958, when Helen Morgan resigns four days after winning the 24th Miss World pageant.
29th	Coco the Clown [Nicolai Poliakoff] special memorial service held at St. Paul's Cathedral, London, England.
30th	"Mack & Mabel" closes at Majestic Theatre NYC after 66 performances.

December

1st — TWA Flight 514, a Boeing 727, crashes 25 miles (40 km) northwest of Dulles International Airport during bad weather, killing all 92 people on board. The same day, in Havershaw, another plane of the same class crashes, causing the death of the three crew members.

2nd — In Addis Ababa, the City Hall and to the Webi Shebeli Hotel are bombed, carried out (according to the international press) by Eritrean nationalists. The Derg (revolutionary council) use the bombings as a pretext for hardened repression against the notables of the negus' regime.

3rd — The Pioneer 11 probe enters the shadow of Jupiter (27,000 miles (43,000 km) from the planet's atmosphere) and captures famous images of the Great Red Spot.

5th — In Argelato (Bologna), the brigadier of carabinieri Andrea Lombardini, in a routine patrol, is murdered with gunfire by five terrorists, who were preparing a robbery on a security officer. The killers, quickly arrested, are members of Lavoro Illegale ("Illegal work"), a terrorist organization come out of Potere Operaio, under the inspiration of Toni Negri, and later merged into the Red brigades. One of them, Bruno Valli, four days later hangs himself in jail. The month in Italy also sees a series of demonstrative attacks by the Red Brigades against industrial managers.

7th — In Arcore, the self-styled prince Luigi D'Angerio, leaving the Silvio Berlusconi's villa, luckily escapes a kidnapping. The probable organizer of the abduction is the Mafioso Vittorio Mangano, Berlusconi's groom, arrested for fraud twenty days later. The episode, never fully explained, will raise many suspicions in the following decades about the presumed links between the Milanese businessman and organized crime.

9th — The Paris summit, reuniting the European Communities' heads of state and government, commences. It states the institution of the European Council and of the ERDF (European regional development fund) and the direct election of the European Parliament by citizens.

10th — The United Nations General Assembly Resolution 3275 declares 1975 International Women's Year.

13th — The United States Congress unanimously approves the Jackson–Vanik amendment, linking the execution of the commercial treaties with Soviet Union to a more liberal politic by Moscow about Jewish emigration.

15th — In Nicaragua, constitution of the UDEL (Union Democratica de Liberacion, Democratic liberation Union), representing the moderate and non-violent wing of the opposition to the Somoza regime.

December

16th — The army of Mali invades the French Upper Volta territory. The border conflict between the two countries will last till 1985.

17th — The United Nations Security Council Resolution 366 terminates South Africa's mandate over Namibia.

20th — In France, Veil law, legalizing abortion, with the favourable vote of UDF and leftist parties and the blackball of UDR.

21st — The New York Times reveals illegal domestic spying by the CIA.

23rd — 37-year-old Karl Brushaber of Ann Arbor, Michigan, falls to his death from the top of Tuckerman Ravine while descending Mount Washington. Brushaber's climbing partner had turned back due to bad weather, but Brushaber pressed on toward the summit; whether or not he reached it is unknown.

24th — Darwin, Australia is almost completely destroyed by Cyclone Tracy.

25th — At the Vatican, Pope Paul VI inaugurates the 1975 Jubilee. During the rite of opening the Holy Door, some falling rubble nearly hits the pontiff.

27th — The Constitutional Court of Italy abolishes the articles of the penal code forbidding strikes for political reasons. The law, enacted by the Fascist regime, was by then mostly no longer applied, though formally in force.

31st — Australian Open Women's Tennis: Australian Evonne Goolagong Cawley retains her title; beats Martina Navratilova of Czechoslovakia 6-3, 6-2

PEOPLE IN POWER

Gough Whitlam
1972-1975
Australia
Prime Minister

Georges Pompidou
1969-1974
France
Président

Emílio Garrastazu Médici
1969-1974
Brazil
President

Pierre Elliott Trudeau
1968-1979
Canada
Prime Minister

Mao Zedong
1943-1976
China
Government of China

Willy Brandt
1969-1974
Germany
President of Germany

Varahagiri Venkata Giri
1969-1974
India
4th President of India

Giovanni Leone
1971-1978
Italy
President

Hiroito
1926-1989
Japan
Emperor

Luis Echeverría
1970-1976
Mexico
President of Mexico

Leonid Brezhnev
1964-1982
Russia
Premier

Jacobus Johannes Fouché
1968-1975
South Africa
Prime Minister

Richard Nixon
1969-1974
United States
President

King Baudouin
1951-1993
Belgium
King

Norman Kirk
1972-1974
New Zealand
Prime Minister

Sir Edward Heath
1970-1974
United Kingdom
Prime Minister

Olof Palme
1969-1976
Sweden
Prime Minister

Poul Hartling
1973-1975
Denmark
Prime Minister

Francisco Franco
1936-1975
Spain
President

János Kádár
1956-1988
Hungary
Hungarian Working
People's Party

The Year You Were Born 1974
Book by Sapphire Publishing
© All rights reserved

Printed in Great Britain
by Amazon